AND BEYOND

Complete
English as a Second Language for Cambridge Secondary 1

Chris Akhurst, Lucy Bowley,
Clare Collinson, Lynette Simonis
Series editor: Rachel Beveridge

ASPIRE
SUCCEED
PROGRESS

8

Oxford excellence for Cambridge Secondary 1

OXFORD

OXFORD
UNIVERSITY PRESS

Great Clarendon Street, Oxford, OX2 6DP, United Kingdom

Oxford University Press is a department of the University of Oxford. It furthers the University's objective of excellence in research, scholarship, and education by publishing worldwide. Oxford is a registered trade mark of Oxford University Press in the UK and in certain other countries

© Oxford University Press 2017

The moral rights of the authors have been asserted

First published in 2017

All rights reserved. No part of this publication may be reproduced, stored in a retrieval system, or transmitted, in any form or by any means, without the prior permission in writing of Oxford University Press, or as expressly permitted by law, by licence or under terms agreed with the appropriate reprographics rights organization. Enquiries concerning reproduction outside the scope of the above should be sent to the Rights Department, Oxford University Press, at the address above.

You must not circulate this work in any other form and you must impose this same condition on any acquirer

British Library Cataloguing in Publication Data
Data available

978-0-19-837813-6

9 10

Paper used in the production of this book is a natural, recyclable product made from wood grown in sustainable forests.
The manufacturing process conforms to the environmental regulations of the country of origin.

Printed and bound by CPI Group (UK) Ltd, Croydon, CR0 4YY

Acknowledgements

The publishers would like to thank the following for permissions to use their photographs:

Cover: Old Havana, Wheatley, Jenny/Private Collection/Bridgeman Images
p8: 123RF; **p10:** 123RF; **p10:** 123RF; **p36:** PYMCA/Getty Images; **p68:** WPA Pool/Pool/Getty Images; **p73:** VikramRaghuvanshi/iStockPhoto; **p89:** Rawpixel/iStockPhoto; **p94:** Natascha Senftleben; **p97:** Mik38/istockPhoto; p100: Hadynyah/iStockPhoto; **p101:** BSIP SA/Alamy Stock Photo; **p105:** Wicki58/iStockPhoto; **p107:** fcafotodigital/Getty Images; **p122:** Chuck Place/Alamy Stock Photo.

All other photos by Shutterstock.

Artwork by Gustavo Berardo and APTARA

We are grateful to the authors and publishers for use of extracts from their titles and in particular for the following:

Julie Angel: *Breaking the Jump*, Published by Aurum Press, London (2016). Reproduced by permission.

W H Auden: "Night Mail" copyright © 1936, renewed 1966 by W. H. Auden; from W. H. AUDEN COLLECTED POEMS. Reprinted by permission of Curtis Brown Ltd.

Jane Austen: Extract from *Emma* retold by Rebecca Stevens, Oxford Reading Tree, Treetops, Greatest Stories (OUP, 2016), copyright © Rebecca Stevens 2016, reprinted by permission of Oxford University Press.

Extract from http://www.hevercastle.co.uk/news/worlds-colourful-5k-run-dye/. Reproduced by permission of The Castle Triathlon Series and Hever Castle.

Stephen Ornes: Cool jobs: Finding foods for the future, 25/09/2015 from https://student.societyforscience.org/article/cool-jobs-finding-foods-future. Reprinted with Permission of Science News for Students.

Verna Wilkins: *Chinwe Roy* – Artist, published by Tamarind. Text © Verna Wilkins. Reprinted by permission of The Random House Group Ltd.

Although we have made every effort to trace and contact all copyright holders before publication this has not been possible in all cases. If notified, the publisher will rectify any errors or omissions at the earliest opportunity.

Links to third party websites are provided by Oxford in good faith and for information only. Oxford disclaims any responsibility for the materials contained in any third party website referenced in this work.

®IGCSE is the registered trademark of Cambridge International Examinations.

All sample questions and answers within this publication have been written by the authors. In examination, the way marks are awarded may be different.

Contents

Introduction 4

Scope and sequence 6

1. Natural landscapes 8

2. Fitness trends 24

3. Working abroad 40

4. Arts and crafts 56

5. Friends and family 72

6. Global learning 88

7. History around us 104

8. Food in the future 120

9. Communication in the past 136

Grammar reference 152

Use of English glossary 156

Index 159

Introduction

Welcome to *Complete English as a Second Language for Cambridge Secondary 1*. This Student Book is the second in a series of three books (Stages 7–9) and is mapped to the *Cambridge Secondary 1* curriculum framework for English as a Second Language.

Who is the book for?

The book has been written for learners of English as a second language and covers all five key skills of the framework: reading, writing, speaking, listening, and use of English. It is designed to meet you where you are and help you improve, with activities that increase gradually in difficulty. It also aims to prepare you to take the Cambridge Secondary 1 Checkpoint test at the end of Stage 9, and then go on to Cambridge IGCSE®.

What is in the book?

The book is divided into nine units, which cover a broad range of fun and interesting topics to give you a wide vocabulary. Each unit includes each of the key skills from the curriculum framework, using the same structure throughout.

Theme opener

Each unit starts with a diagram like the one below, which will show what is covered in that unit.

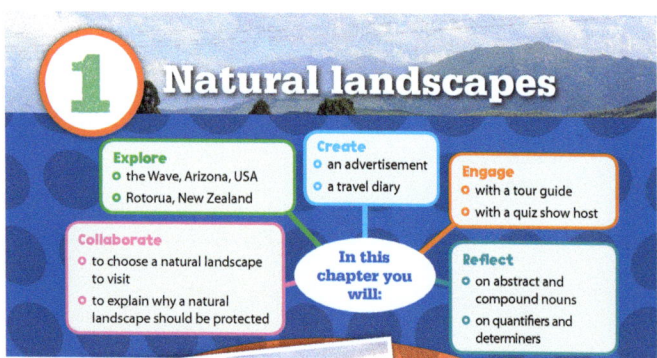

Photos and quotes help you to start thinking and talking about the topic, building some of the vocabulary that you will need throughout the unit.

 ## Reading

You will find a broad range of writing styles and registers. Each text is followed by questions to make sure you have understood the text.

At the end of each unit, you will also find a 'Reading corner', which will introduce you to a slightly longer and more challenging text. This is designed to give you an appreciation of English in many different contexts and to help model good writing skills.

Use of English

You will find two sections on the use of English in each unit: these include short explanations on the grammar and punctuation rules that you will need to know, followed by activities to put into practice what you have learned.

 ## Listening

Listening activities include different styles of talk and conversation, followed by questions, to help develop your understanding of spoken English. The audio recordings are on the CD in your book where you can also find transcripts (or the 'text' of what you hear) for extra help.

Speaking

You will have the chance to practise your speaking skills, both in groups and on your own. There will usually be a picture or photo, followed by discussion questions, to help get you started.

 ## Writing

Short writing activities are scattered throughout the book and each unit includes one 'Writing workshop' in which you complete an extended piece of writing (100–120 words). This covers many different types of writing, such as stories, letters, reports and blogs.

Progress assessment

Each unit ends with a Progress check, a quick test to make sure that you have remembered what you learned in the unit. This is followed by a Progress assessment grid and an Action plan to help you decide where you need to improve.

Other features

 ## World builder

Word builder: activities to help you understand and practise using difficult words.

 ## Remember

Short tips to remind you of things you have already learned, that will help you to complete the activities.

 ## Challenge

If you are feeling confident, the stretching Challenge activities provide extra practice.

 ## Suggested reading

If you like the extracts in the 'Reading corner', you will find suggestions for other texts that you might like.

Glossary

Really difficult words will have a definition (in English) to help you understand the text or listening task.

And finally…

We have included a very wide range of themes, texts and listening scenarios so we hope you will find this book interesting and engaging, as you grow into confident, responsible, reflective, innovative and engaged learners of English. Good luck!

Unit contents

Unit	Theme	Reading and comprehension	Listening and comprehension
1	Natural landscapes	Non-fiction: Different landscapes Non-fiction: Travel diary	Quiz show host asks questions about the Sahara Desert Tour guide talks about the Wave in Arizona
2	Fitness trends	Non-fiction: Article about a colour run Factual novel: *Breaking the Jump*	Fitness coach talks about a colour run Three boys discuss fitness classes at their local sports centre
3	Working abroad	Ji-Min's story Newspaper article: Working abroad	Silas talks about moving to a different country for work
4	Arts and crafts	Instructions: Paper basket weaving Biography: *Artist*	An entrepreneur talks about how her hobby became her business
5	Friends and family	Letters between a student and her grandmother Fiction: *Emma*	Three friends discuss families
6	Global learning	Non-fiction: How e-books can help to make a global community Non-fiction: Article to persuade	Interview with a young e-author (Harrison Wallace)
7	History around us	Non-fiction: Paper, pens and pencils Poetry: 'Light bulb'	A group of friends discuss the invention of light bulbs
8	Food in the future	Non-fiction: Finding foods for the future Blog and a diary entry	Two chefs from the future discuss their menu
9	Communication in the past	Non-ficton: Pigeon post Poetry: 'The Postage Stamp Lesson'	A salesperson talks about the historic typewriters he has for sale Reading of the poem 'The Night Mail'

Language, grammar, spelling, vocabulary	Writing	Speaking
Abstract and compound nouns Countable and uncountable nouns Determiners Quantifiers	Non-fiction: Writing an advertisement Non-fiction: Writing a travel diary	Expressing and giving reasons for opinions Devising a spoken advertisement Using formal and informal language Negotiating classroom tasks Using subject-specific vocabulary
Adjectives Making comparisons Adverbs in sentences	Writing an email Writing a factual story	Expressing and giving reasons for opinions Using subject-specific vocabulary Designing a poster to persuade Using questions to check understanding
Demonstrative and indefinite pronouns Reflexive pronouns Prepositions	Writing an informal email Writing an advertisement to persuade Writing a formal email Writing a job application	Expressing and giving reasons for opinions Giving a class talk Talking about advantages and disadvantages
Active and passive forms Causative forms Present continuous Past continuous	Writing a formal letter Writing to summarise someone's opinion Writing a biography	Expressing opinions Role playing and using language to persuade Talking about advantages and disadvantages Using subject-specific vocabulary Group presentation
Questions Reported statements, commands and questions Indirect and embedded questions	Writing a letter to a relative Writing summaries and descriptions Fiction: Writing a story about meeting someone for the first time	Expressing opinions Using subject-specific vocabulary Using questions to check understanding Group discussion and presentation
Present perfect Past perfect –ing forms used as nouns Noun phrases	Writing a formal email Fiction: Writing the first paragraph and designing the cover for an e-book Non-fiction: Writing an article to persuade	Expressing and giving reasons for opinions Giving a short presentation Using subject-specific vocabulary Negotiating classroom tasks Group research and presentation
Conjunctions Infinitives after adjectives and verbs Verbs + –ing forms	Non-fiction: Writing about an everyday object Poetry: Writing an acrostic poem	Expressing ideas and opinions Using subject-specific vocabulary
Talking about the future Modal verbs	Writing a review of a meal from the future Fiction: Writing the beginning of a story, *The Great Hunger of 2040* Writing two imaginative blogs	Expressing ideas and opinions Adapting language where there are gaps in knowledge Using subject-specific vocabulary Class competition to design an advertisement
'If only' and 'wish' Relative pronouns and relative clauses Phrasal verbs Prepositional verbs	Non-fiction: Writing about sending messages in the past Poetry: Writing a lesson poem Poetry: Writing based on 'The Night Mail'	Expressing opinions and ideas Negotiating classroom tasks Class presentation Using subject-specific vocabulary

1 Natural landscapes

Explore
- the Wave, Arizona, USA
- Rotorua, New Zealand

Create
- an advertisement
- a travel diary

Engage
- with a tour guide
- with a quiz show host

Collaborate
- to choose a natural landscape to visit
- to explain why a natural landscape should be protected

In this chapter you will:

Reflect
- on abstract and compound nouns
- on quantifiers and determiners

Nature is so powerful, so strong.
Annie Liebovitz, photographer

The true miracle is not walking on water or walking in air, but simply walking on this earth. Thich Nhat Hanh, Buddhist monk and teacher

Lose yourself in nature and find peace.
Ralph Waldo Emerson, poet

8

Natural landscapes

Thinking ahead

1. How many kinds of natural landscapes can you think of?
2. Why are natural landscapes pleasant to visit?
3. Should we ever change the way natural landscapes look?

Word builder

1. Match the word on the left with the definition on the right. The first one has been done for you.

unspoilt	still in a natural state
remote	a long way from where people live
undeveloped	without anyone living there
unexplored	not damaged by humans
uninhabited	not investigated by humans

   (unspoilt — not damaged by humans)

2. Which of these sentences use the words from question 1 correctly and which do not? Rewrite any sentences that are not correct.

   a The woodland is completely <u>unspoilt</u>, as it has been the same for over 10,000 years.

   b The mountains are so <u>remote</u> that it is really easy to walk to them.

   c People have travelled all over the world so there are very few places that are still <u>unexplored</u>.

   d There were a few hundred people living on the small <u>uninhabited</u> island.

   e The fields near my home are <u>undeveloped</u>, but that is likely to change soon.

Speaking about landscapes

Which of the different landscapes you thought of in the Thinking ahead activity would you most like to photograph? Work with a partner to tell each other which you would photograph and why.

> **Remember**
>
> When you discuss your opinions with your partner, try to use some of the words from the Word builder activity.

Reading

 Different landscapes

Read these descriptions of four natural landscapes.

Great Barrier Reef, Australia

The Great Barrier Reef is off the east coast of Australia. It is a stretch of **coral** covering over 344,000 square kilometres (about the same size as Japan or Germany). The area gives visitors the chance to swim or scuba dive and see the coral as well as colourful fish.

Victoria Falls, Zambia-Zimbabwe border

Victoria Falls, a waterfall on the Zambezi River, is 1,600 metres wide and 108 metres high. This makes the water flow over the top a spectacular sight. The noise and the **spray** created by the force of the water are incredible, so it is no surprise that the waterfall is also known as 'The Smoke that Thunders'.

Atacama Desert, Chile

The Atacama Desert in Chile is the driest hot desert in the world, There is often less than 1 millimetre of rain per year; some places in the desert have never recorded any rain. Parts of the desert have been compared to the surface of Mars, so maybe living there would be a bit like living on Mars!

Lake Baikal, Siberia

At 1,632 metres deep, Lake Baikal is the world's deepest lake and it contains 20% of the world's unfrozen water. It is also the world's oldest freshwater lake, between 20 and 25 million years old. Many of the plants and animals that live there – such as the freshwater seal – are only found in this lake.

> **Glossary**
> **coral** a hard substance made by a sea animal
> **spray** tiny drops of liquid blown through the air

Reading

Understanding

A Choose the correct answer to the following questions.

1. Which country is about the same size as the Great Barrier Reef?
   - a Germany
   - b Australia
   - c Chile

2. Why do you think Victoria Falls is known as 'The Smoke That Thunders'?
   - a It produces a lot of smoke.
   - b There is thunder around the waterfall.
   - c The water produces spray that looks like smoke and the noise is as loud as thunder.

3. Give a reason why the Atacama Desert has been compared to Mars.
   - a Some parts have never had any water.
   - b It is red.
   - c It is 105 square kilometres.

4. How much of the world's unfrozen water is in Lake Baikal?
   - a $\frac{1}{3}$
   - b $\frac{1}{4}$
   - c $\frac{1}{5}$

B Read what the four tourists below say. Each tourist would most like to visit one of the natural landscapes on page 10. Match each tourist with a landscape.

Sabera: I like travelling to different landscapes, but only to see them and not get too involved. I love water.

Max: I am a film actor and director and love sci-fi in particular, so I would like to travel to a landscape that could be on a different planet!

Chet: I love swimming in the sea. I have been snorkelling a few times but I would like to go scuba diving in a natural place one day.

Ava: I like being on the water, but not particularly underneath it – I am happy staying in a boat. I don't enjoy being in warm climates.

C Which of the landscapes on page 10 would you choose to visit and why? Explain your answer to a partner.

Challenge

Track 1.1 You are going to listen to a quiz show. Kiril is answering questions about a natural landscape. Listen to the quiz and then answer these questions.

1. In square kilometres, how big is the Sahara Desert?
2. Name a country that includes part of the Sahara Desert.
3. What is most of the Sahara made of?
4. Which animal is the jerboa related to?
5. How does the jerboa keep cool?

Use of English

Abstract nouns and compound nouns

Abstract nouns name ideas, qualities, feelings and concepts.

Examples: belief, thought, beauty

Many abstract nouns are formed by adding suffixes to verbs or adjectives. We often add –ment, –ion, –tion, –ation and –sion to verbs. The suffixes –ness, –ity, –ance and –ence are often added to adjectives. Sometimes the spelling of the original word changes when we add the suffix.

Examples: appoint → appoint**ment**   discuss → discuss**ion**   examine → examin**ation**
kind → kind**ness**   act**ive** → activ**ity**   differ**ent** → differ**ence**

Compound nouns are made up of two or more words. Compound nouns may be made from different parts of speech. Some common examples are:

- **noun + noun**   *Example*: sun + glasses = sunglasses
- **adjective + noun**   *Example*: full + moon = full moon
- **noun + verb(–ing)**   *Examples*: sun + rise = sunrise   horse + riding = horse riding

Using abstract and compound nouns

A Answer the following questions.

1. Complete the following sentences with abstract nouns formed from the words in brackets.
   - a Our guide gave us lots of _____. (inform)
   - b Before _____ fell, we saw a spectacular sunset. (dark)
   - c The rain didn't spoil our _____. (enjoy)

2. Make as many compound nouns as you can from the words in the box.

scuba	water	storm	fall
rain	diving	drop	thunder

B Find the five abstract nouns and the five compound nouns in the following paragraph.

Diary

I felt such excitement as we approached the waterfall. When we finally arrived, the power of the water was a huge surprise. Wearing my waterproof raincoat and strong walking shoes, I stood on the slippery footpath. I watched in amazement, felt the spray and took photos of a beautiful rainbow. This was an adventure I will never forget!

Remember

- Suffixes are letters added to the end of words to make new words.
- Some compound nouns are written as one word. Others are written as two words and some are written with a hyphen.

Examples: bedroom, tennis ball, great-grandmother

Use of English

Countable and uncountable nouns

Countable nouns refer to things that we can count. Most countable nouns can be singular or plural.

Examples: a **lake**, two **waterfalls**

Uncountable nouns refer to things we cannot count. For example:

- substances and materials such as 'bread', 'water', 'cotton' and 'air'
- abstract ideas and concepts such as 'knowledge' and 'advice'
- weather words such as 'thunder', 'rain' and 'snow'
- activities such as 'tennis', 'swimming' and 'sleep'.

Most uncountable nouns do not have a plural form. We cannot say 'advices'.

Some nouns can be countable and uncountable, depending on how they are used.

Examples: I put a **glass** on the table. (countable)
This table is made of **glass**. (uncountable)

Using countable and uncountable nouns

A Make two lists with the headings 'Countable' and 'Uncountable'. Put the nouns from the shopping list below in the correct list.

Shopping list

salt	spinach	eggs	oranges
toothpaste	milk	carrots	sun cream
onions	potatoes	tomatoes	shampoo

B Find the eight mistakes in this email and then rewrite the email correctly.

Dear tour guide

I am planning some trip to the Atacama Desert. Please can you send me an information about the sceneries in the area? What are the weathers like? Are there any wildlife? Will I need to take a warm clothing for night-time? Is it a good place for activities such as campings?

C Use each noun below in two sentences of your own. In the first, use the word as a countable noun. In the second, use it as an uncountable noun.

room   chocolate   time

Remember

- We can use 'a/an' and 'the' with singular countable nouns and 'the', 'some' and 'any' with plural countable nouns.

- With uncountable nouns, we cannot use 'a/an' but we can use 'the', 'some' and 'any'.

- When we use a singular noun we use a singular verb. With plural nouns, we use plural verbs.

13

Listening

The Wave, Arizona

 Word builder

Match the words and phrases on the left with the correct meanings on the right.

Arizona	a type of rock that is often yellow, red or brown
decade	skills someone has been taught
sandstone	walking for a long distance across country
spectacular	one of the 50 states in the USA, in the west of the country
hiking	ten years
training	very exciting or surprising

 Track 1.2 Tour guide

You are going to listen to a tour guide, who is talking about the Wave, a natural landscape made of sandstone in Arizona. Listen carefully and then answer the questions on page 15.

14

Listening

Understanding

A Choose the correct answer to the following questions.

1. How did the tourists get tickets to go to the Wave?
   a They bought them that morning.
   b They won them.
   c They bought them online.
2. What did the tourists travel along to reach the Wave?
   a the Rock Rough Road
   b the Wave Valley Road
   c the House Rock Valley Road
3. How old is the sandstone found at the Wave?
   a 140 years old
   b a million years old
   c over 140 million years old

B Answer the following questions.

1. What made the spectacular patterns in the rock?
2. Name two specific things you could photograph at the Wave.
3. What should the tourists do if they feel unwell?

C Answer the following questions.

1. How have tourist numbers changed over the past few decades?
2. Why do you think the guide told them to check their shoes were tied and their water bottles were full?
3. How would you feel if you were just about to start this tour?

Speaking: One-minute call

Imagine you have been on the tour of the Wave. Now you are allowed to make a one-minute call. Who would you call to talk about the tour and what would you say? Work with a partner to take turns speaking for one minute about the Wave.

Use of English

Determiners

Determiners are words that come at the beginning of a noun phrase.

Specific determiners	General determiners
the, this, that, these, those, my, your, his, her, its, our, their, whose, which	a/an, another, any, other, what

We use specific determiners to refer to a particular person or thing. We use general determiners when we are being less specific.

Examples: I shall buy **that** guidebook before we go.   Did you see **any** interesting places?

We often use 'half (of)', 'both (of)' and 'all (of)' before determiners.

Example: **Half of the** visitors found the dinosaur prints.

To add more meaning, we use words such as 'quite', 'such' and 'what' before 'a/an'.

Examples: It was **quite a** nice day.   It was **such an** exciting trip.   **What a** fantastic place!

Using determiners

A Find all the determiners in the following sentences.

1. Which shoes should I take – my boots or these sandals?
2. Before our hike, the guide gave us a map and told us about other interesting places nearby.
3. The best time to take photos of the Wave is at midday when there aren't any shadows.

B Use words from the box to complete Kai's email.

> quite   such   what   the   those   that

Hi Sandro

We had _____ a wonderful trip to _____ Wave!
We stayed in _____ little hotel you mentioned. It was a hot day, so the walk was _____ a challenge.
We found _____ dinosaur prints you told us about.
_____ an amazing sight!

Kai

Remember

A noun phrase is a group of words that includes a noun and other words that give more information about the noun.

Example: your new walking boots

C Write three sentences of your own using the following phrases: 'half of his', 'both your' and 'all the'.

16

Use of English

Quantifiers

Quantifiers are determiners that give information about how many there are or how much there is of something.

With countable and uncountable nouns	Only with countable nouns	Only with uncountable nouns
all, some, plenty of, a lot of, lots of, more, most, enough, no, none of	both, each, either, every, (a) few, fewer, many, neither, several, hundreds of, thousands of, millions of, a couple of, a dozen, a large/small number of	much, (a) little, less, a bit of, a large/small amount of, a great deal of

When we want to be more exact about how much there is of an uncountable noun, we can use phrases such as 'a piece of', 'a tube of', 'a glass of', 'a cup of', 'a bottle of', 'a slice of', 'a litre of' and 'a bar of'.

Example: Please could we have **two glasses of** orange juice?

Using quantifiers

A Fill the gaps with the correct word from the brackets.

1. There wasn't _____ accommodation in the area. (much/many)
2. I took two guidebooks, but I didn't use _____ of them. (neither/either)
3. They had _____ time for sightseeing. (few/little)

B Correct the mistakes in the following sentences.

1. He had already been to Arizona several of times.
2. I knew I'd be thirsty, so I took two bottle of waters.
3. How many piece of luggages do you have?

C Fill the gaps in the following paragraph with a suitable quantifier.

Our tour guide gave us _____ information about the rocks. He told us that the sandstone dates back _____ years. They don't allow _____ people to visit _____ day. We didn't have _____ time to explore _____ part of the area, so _____ of us want to go back.

> **Remember**
>
> We usually put 'of' after quantifiers that are followed by a determiner or a pronoun.
>
> *Examples*: We saw most of the best places in the area. A few of us saw the dinosaur prints.

Speaking

Describing natural landscapes

Look at the photographs of natural landscapes and then carry out the activities that follow.

💬 Describing natural landscapes

1. Think of two adjectives to describe the landscape in each of the photographs above. Then tell your partner which adjectives you have chosen. Decide on the two best ones for each photo.

2. Now join with another pair to discuss which of these landscapes you would most like to visit. Give reasons for your choice and try to use interesting adjectives to describe the landscape.

Speaking

 ## Word builder

1. Match the word on the left with the definition on the right.

protect	the air, land and water where animals and plants live
scenery	attractive natural things you see in the countryside
surroundings	very good or very beautiful
environment	the conditions around a place or person
magnificent	keep something safe

2. Use each of the words above in the following sentences.
   a The mountains were huge and _____.
   b I enjoyed visiting the lake, but the _____ were not so pleasant.
   c The nature group wanted to _____ the local _____.
   d I decided to try and paint the beautiful _____.

 ## Create an advertisement

You are going to work in small groups to write and present an advertisement explaining why your chosen natural landscape should be protected.

First, decide in your group where the natural landscape is (country and area) and include details about what the landscape is made of and how it was formed. Each person in the group can research the landscape on the Internet and then contribute one fact about it for the advertisement.

In your group, decide on the order you want to present these facts. When you have agreed the order, think of at least two reasons why the natural landscape is so special and why it should be protected.

Finally, decide who will write the advertisement and who will present it – make sure everyone in the group has a chance to take part.

 **Remember**

You can use the informal register when discussing ideas in your group, but you should use formal language when you present your advertisement to the class.

Reading corner

 Reading corner: Travel diary

Read the following extract from a travel diary written by a tourist who has been visiting Rotorua in New Zealand.

I am in the town of Rotorua, which is part of the Taupo Volcanic Zone in the centre of the North Island in New Zealand. I have been here for three days and I have to write down how I feel about it because it isn't like any place I've ever been to before.

There are many **geothermal** features here – why didn't I listen a bit more carefully to Miss Swann in all of those geography lessons? What I have learned is that the land is **volcanic** and there are lakes, **geysers** that send hot water into the air, mud pools and colourful **terraces**. All together they make an amazing sight. Visitors have been coming here for over 200 years. My favourite geyser is the Pohutu geyser, which **erupts** up to 20 times a day and has always been popular with tourists. It's actually really noisy with the sound of the mud pools and the geysers – people are always surprised when the hot water comes up. The strangest thing about Rotorua though is the smell. Everywhere smells of old eggs because of all the yellow sulphur. You can see yellow patches all along the roads.

Tomorrow, I am going to Waimangu Volcanic Valley, which is the youngest geothermal **ecosystem** in the world. I have packed my walking boots and am going to try to sleep tonight, but it is going to be hard because I am really excited!

Understanding

Answer the following questions.

1. In which country is Rotorua?
2. Give two examples of natural features you can see in Rotorua.
3. For how long Rotorua been a tourist area?
4. What does the writer say the most unusual thing about Rotorua is?
5. Write down what you would like to visit on a trip to Rotorua and why.

Glossary

ecosystem the animals and plants that live together in one place

erupts bursts through

geothermal to do with the heat inside the Earth

geyser natural hot water that comes up through rock

terraces different levels

volcanic adjective describing land near or caused by a volcano

Writing workshop

 Writing a travel diary

You are going to write a travel diary about a natural landscape of your choice.

Planning

First choose a natural landscape to write about. This could be somewhere near where you live or somewhere you would like to visit. Do some research to find out more about the place you have chosen.

A travel diary has a mixture of fact and opinion, so you need to include details about the place you are visiting as well as giving your opinion about it. Imagine you are standing in the natural landscape right now. Write a sentence giving at least one fact about the place and then another expressing how you feel.

A travel diary uses informal language, so contractions (for example 'won't' rather than 'will not') are allowed. What other features of informal language can you think of? Work with a partner to make a list.

Writing, editing and proofreading

Now write your travel diary. Remember to include some facts and also your feelings about it. Write about 100 words.

Once you have written your travel diary, give it to your partner, who will proofread it and give you some feedback on it.

> **Remember**
>
> A proofreader should check that:
> - the piece of writing has the right register and layout (for example laid out like a travel diary and written in informal language)
> - the content has answered the question
> - spelling, punctuation and grammar are accurate.

Progress assessment

Progress check

Answer the following questions.

1. Write three sentences. Each sentence should include one of the words in the box.

   uninhabited   scenery   unspoilt

   (3 marks)

2. Which two items would you take on a trip to the Victoria Falls? Write a paragraph of 50–70 words to explain why you have chosen each item. (4 marks)

3. Name an animal that you might find in Lake Baikal in Siberia. (1 mark)

4. There is one mistake in each of the following sentences. Rewrite each sentence correctly.
   a Our tour guide gave us some excellent advices about places to visit.
   b We had such a terrible weather when we went to Australia. (2 marks)

5. Think of three adjectives you could use to describe the Wave. (3 marks)

6. Give one word to describe a period of ten years. (1 mark)

7. Which **two** of these sentences are correct?
   a Either of us have been to New Zealand.
   b Both of them have been to New Zealand.
   c Neither of us has been to New Zealand. (2 marks)

8. Which **two** of the following statements are true?
   a Rotorua is in South Island, New Zealand.
   b Rotorua smells of old eggs.
   c People have visited Rotorua for hundreds of years. (2 marks)

9. Explain what a geyser is and where you could see one. (2 marks)

10. Write a travel diary entry explaining why a natural landscape of your choice should be protected. Write 50–70 words. (5 marks)

(Total: 25 marks)

Progress assessment

Progress assessment

		😊	😐	😟
Reading skills	I can understand the main point in a text.	○	○	○
	I can understand specific points in a text.	○	○	○
Use of English skills	I can use abstract and compound nouns.	○	○	○
	I can use quantifiers and determiners.	○	○	○
Listening skills	I can understand the main points that someone is saying.	○	○	○
	I can understand most of the specific points that someone is saying.	○	○	○
Speaking skills	I can explain my own point of view.	○	○	○
	I can use formal and informal language.	○	○	○
	I can work with others to agree and organise ways to complete tasks.	○	○	○
Writing skills	I can brainstorm, plan and draft written work with some support.	○	○	○
	I can write, edit and proofread written work with some support.	○	○	○

✓ Action plan

Reading: I need to _____

Use of English: I need to _____

Listening: I need to _____

Speaking: I need to _____

Writing: I need to _____

I would like to know more about _____

2 Fitness trends

Explore
- colour running
- parkour

Create
- a poster
- a factual story

Engage
- with three students
- with a fitness coach

Collaborate
- to design a poster
- to discuss past and present fitness trends

In this chapter you will:

Reflect
- on adjectives
- on adverbs

A fit healthy body – that is the best fashion statement. Jess C Scott, writer

Focus on progress, not perfection. Josh Bezoni, nutritionist and fitness expert

The difference between try and triumph is a little umph. Marvin Phillips, basketball player

Fitness trends

Thinking ahead

A fitness trend is a popular and often new way to keep fit. A fitness trend can last for one season or for several years.

1. What fitness trends have you heard of?
2. Have you ever tried any? If so, which?
3. Would you try a new fitness trend if you had the chance? Would it make a difference if you did not have to buy anything to try it? Explain your answer.

Word builder

Look at the six fitness trends below. Match the name on the left with the definition on the right.

aerobics	dancing to jazz music
pilates	moving while holding two sticks as if playing the drums
zumba	exercising while standing on a moving plate
jazzercise	moving to music, often with hand weights
fitness plate	making smooth movements to make the body stronger and more flexible (able to bend)
drum sticks	dancing to Latin American and popular music

Speaking about fitness trends

Which of the fitness trends above would you most like to do? Tell your partner which one you have chosen and why.

Then discuss why taking up a new fitness trend might encourage you to get fit or stay fit. Use the words and phrases from the word box to help you.

haven't done it before	never tried it before
fun interesting	popular trendy cool

25

Reading

Colour run

Read this extract from a web page, which is about a growing running trend – colour running.

World's most colourful 5K – Run or Dye

This is your chance to have THE most colour-filled day of your life with family and friends as you celebrate life, friendship, fitness and fun.

What it's like

… As you run/walk/dance through the course, you will get showered in safe, **eco-friendly,** plant-based powdered dye at every kilometre… turning you into a **technicolour canvas** of fun!

Just when you thought you couldn't possibly be more colourful, you'll cross the finish line and find yourself in the middle of a colourstorm at our Finish Festival! … The result is a once-in-a-lifetime experience that many people tell us is the most fun they've ever had exercising.

Who should come

Run or Dye is for absolutely everyone! … You're welcome to walk, run, dance, or skip your way to the finish line. And Run or

Dye is family-friendly — **kids** 6 and under run FREE!

What to wear

At Run or Dye, YOU are the canvas, so wear whatever you want! Lots of runners prefer wearing white to show off all the colour… but many come dressed in crazy costumes, like an old wedding dress, pirate outfit, or those leopard-print pyjamas. While the dye is designed to be washable, we don't do your **laundry**, so we recommend that you wear something you don't mind getting a little colourful.

Glossary

canvas cloth that artists paint on
eco-friendly something that will not harm the environment
kids children
laundry washing clothes
technicolour brightly coloured

Reading

Understanding

A Choose the correct answer to each of the following questions.

1. Which of the following best describes Run or Dye?
   a a celebration of flowers and friendship
   b a celebration of fitness and fun
   c a celebration of family and friends
2. Who can go on a colour run?
   a anyone
   b families with children under six only
   c anyone who can run the whole way round
3. Why might someone wear white clothes to Run or Dye?
   a to keep their clothes clean
   b to show off the dye
   c because they want to wash their clothes

B Answer the following questions.

1. Does it cost any money to do a colour run? Choose the correct answer.
   a No, it is free.
   b Yes, everyone has to pay.
   c Some people have to pay.
2. What makes a colour run different from a normal run?
3. What does the article mean by saying 'YOU are the canvas'?
4. Write at least two benefits of taking part in a colour run.

C Answer the following questions.

1. What would you say to a friend to persuade them to take part in a colour run? Turn to your partner and persuade them to run with you in the next colour run.
2. Imagine you have been on a colour run. Write a short email to a friend telling them what happened and how you felt about taking part. Write 40–60 words.

Challenge

Track 2.1 You are going to listen to a fitness coach who has organised a colour run at your school. Listen and then answer these questions.

1. Why does the coach say students should take part in the colour run?
2. What does the coach suggest students wear to the colour run?
3. When will the school colour run take place?
4. What item must students bring with them on the colour run?
5. Why do you think the coach tells them to bring this item?

Use of English

Adjectives

We often use two or more words together to make a **compound adjective**. We usually put a hyphen between the words.

Example: The colour run is a **five-kilometre** run.

Many adjectives end in **–ing** or **–ed**. They have the same form as present or past participles.

We often use adjectives ending in –ed to describe feelings. Adjectives ending in –ing are usually used to describe the person or thing that causes the feelings.

Examples: I feel very **excited** about the run.
The run is very **exciting**.

For spelling rules when adding –ing or –ed to verbs, see page 153.

 **Remember**

Compound adjectives are often used to describe:

- someone's appearance or character
  Examples: curly-haired, easy-going

- the appearance of places and things.
  Examples: run-down, multi-coloured, blue-green

Using adjectives

A Answer these questions.

1. Fill the gaps in the sentences with compound adjectives formed from words in the box.

   | tempered   child   long   friendly   bad   distance |

   a They ran for over 20 kilometres. It was a _____ race.
   b He is always getting annoyed. He is very _____.
   c My little brother can take part because the colour run is very _____.

2. Fill the gaps with an –ing or –ed form of the verbs in brackets.

   a I was _____ that I couldn't take part. (disappoint)
   b A few runners were _____ about the route and went the wrong way. (confuse)
   c Some children found the run quite _____. (tire)

B Find the –ing or –ed adjective in each of the following sentences.

1. I am hoping to take part – the colour run sounds amazing.
2. Kris is resting today because he is exhausted.
3. Lara had arrived early, so she felt very relaxed.

Challenge

Find six compound adjectives in the text on page 26. Then choose three of the adjectives and use them in sentences of your own.

28

Use of English

Making comparisons

We use **comparative adjectives** followed by 'than' to compare two things.

Examples: Tarek is **taller than** Ali. Is zumba **more popular than** aerobics?

To compare two things that are the same, we often use 'as … as' or 'just as … as'.

Examples: Pasha is **as tall as** Farah. Aerobics is **just as popular as** zumba.

To say that someone or something is 'less', we use 'not so/as … as' or 'less … than'.

Examples: Ali is **not as tall as** Tarek. Jazzercise is **less popular than** zumba.

To make a comparison stronger or weaker, we can use words and phrases such as 'much', 'a bit', 'far', 'a lot', 'slightly', 'a little' and 'nowhere near as … as'.

Example: I find aerobics **far more tiring** than swimming.

We use **superlative adjectives** to express the idea of 'most' or 'least'.

Examples: Rania is the **tallest** student in the class.
The colour run is the **most colourful** run in the world.

Using comparative and superlative adjectives

> **Remember**
>
> If an adjective has one syllable, we usually add –er to make a comparative and –est to make a superlative. We usually use 'more' or 'most' if an adjective has two syllables or more.
>
> See page 152 for more on forming comparative and superlative adjectives.

A Fill the gaps in the following sentences with the correct comparative or superlative form of the adjective in brackets.

1. I am pleased with my new trainers. They are _____ than my old ones. (comfortable)
2. They said yesterday was the _____ day of the year. (hot)
3. Of all the runs I have done, I found the colour run the _____. (enjoyable)

B Use the following words to write comparative or superlative sentences.

1. football/running/fun/a lot
2. Kara/old/as/not/Gleb
3. aerobics/easy/far/think/pilates
4. fast/runner/whole school/Ammar

C Write three sentences of your own using a comparative phrase on the left with the correct form of any of the adjectives on the right.

a bit …	challenging
just as …	strong
a lot …	cheap

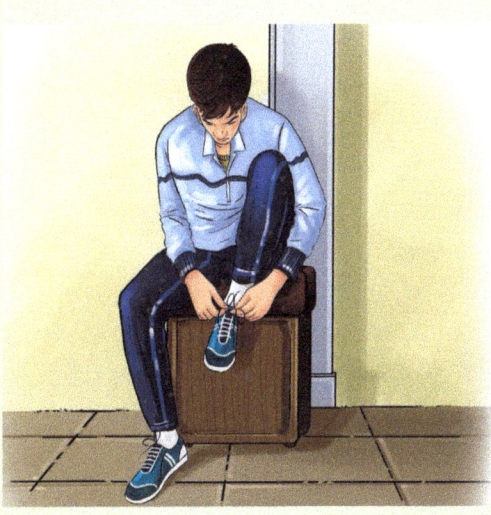

Listening

Choosing a fitness trend

 Word builder

Rewrite the sentences, filling the gaps with the correct words from the word box.

| app | yoga | middle-aged | athlete |

1. Hannah does a _____ class because it makes her feel calmer and fitter.
2. The Paralympic swimmer was a superb _____.
3. Ivo downloaded an _____ to record how far he walked in a day.
4. My aunty, who is _____, really enjoys her zumba class.

 Track 2.2: New fitness activities

The three boys in the recording are using a fitness app to find out more information about new classes that are being held at the sports centre. Listen to their conversation and then answer the questions on page 31.

Listening

Understanding

A Choose the correct answer to each of the following questions.

1. Which fitness activity has the sports centre offered for some time?
   a yoga
   b pilates
   c yogalates

2. Which fitness activity is new to the sports centre?
   a karate
   b zumba
   c capoeira

3. What type of activity is spinning?
   a running
   b cycling
   c dance

B Answer these questions.

1. How do the students find out about the new fitness trends at their sports centre?
2. What is yogalates?
3. Do they like the idea of capoeira or not? Give a reason for your answer.

C Answer these questions.

1. Which fitness activity do the students choose?
2. Why do they choose this activity? How do you know?
3. Why do you think the three boys like trying out new fitness trends?

 Speaking: What do you think?

Which fitness activity mentioned in the recording would you choose and why? Discuss your ideas with your partner.

31

Use of English

Adverbs in sentences

Adverbs that tell us how, where or when something happens usually come after the main verb or at the end of a clause or sentence.

Examples:
We waited **patiently** for the class to start.   It was raining **yesterday**, so I stayed **inside**.

Adverbs that tell us how often something happens or how certain something is usually come before the main verb.

Examples: I **always** walk to school.   She is **probably** going to be late.

We sometimes use adverbs at the beginning of a sentence to add an opinion or comment about the whole sentence. These are called 'sentence adverbs'.

Example: **Unfortunately**, I was late for the class.

Some sentence adverbs come at the end of a sentence.

Examples:

I don't like athletics. I like football, **though**. (= but I like football)

I love aerobics. I like running **as well**. (= I also like running)

Using adverbs in sentences

A Rewrite the sentences, putting the adverbs in brackets in the most suitable position.

1. The boys go to the sports centre together. (regularly)
2. They thought about which class to do. (carefully)
3. The sports centre holds yoga classes. It holds spinning classes. (as well)
4. They all wanted to do the same class. (luckily)

B Fill the gaps in the conversation with suitable adverbs or adverbial phrases from the word box.

| always | probably | then | as well |
| yesterday | tomorrow | after school | though |

Diego: Did you book the spinning class _____?
Leo: Yes. They want us to pay some money, _____. They said people _____ have to pay first. We have to fill some forms in _____.
Diego: We should _____ go to the sports centre _____.
Leo: Shall we go _____?
Diego: Yes, great. See you _____.

> **Remember**
> When a verb has an object, we usually put the adverb after the object.
> *Example:* He read the instructions carefully.

Use of English

Making comparisons

With short adverbs, such as 'fast', 'hard', 'early' or 'late', we add –er to make a **comparative adverb** and –est to make a **superlative**.

Examples: Jonas arrived **later** than Gaurav. Ali arrived **latest**.

If an adverb has two or more syllables, we usually use 'more' or 'less' to make a comparative. We use '(the) most' or '(the) least' to make a superlative.

Examples:

Jonas plays football **less often** than Gaurav.   Ali plays **(the) least frequently**.

Some adverbs have irregular comparative and superlative forms.

Examples:

well ⟶ better ⟶ best   badly ⟶ worse ⟶ worst

far ⟶ farther/further ⟶ farthest/furthest

Using comparative and superlative adverbs

A Complete these sentences with a comparative or superlative form of the adverb in brackets.

1. I go swimming far _____ than I used to. (regularly)
2. Ava is very fit. Of all the students in the school, she can run _____. (fast)
3. Nada said she would arrive _____ than me. (early)
4. Ranim is trying to eat _____. (healthily)

B Rewrite the following sentences correcting the mistakes.

1. Jamal is working much more hardly this term.
2. I play lots of sports, but the one I play the more often is tennis.
3. Rania did much worst in her exams than she was expecting.
4. Sara played just as well than she did last week.

C Write three sentences using one of the phrases on the left with one of the adverbs on the right.

far	politely
just as	quietly
slightly	early

Remember

We can use words and phrases such as 'as … as', 'just as … as', 'far', 'much' and 'a bit' with comparative adverbs.

Example: Jima can run just as fast as Lucia.

See page 152 for more information on how to form comparative and superlative adverbs.

Speaking

 ## Designing a poster

You are part of a team responsible for encouraging more young people to attend their local sports centre. The team needs to attract more students as you have heard that several are now going to the new sports centre on the other side of your town.

Work together to discuss:

- new classes that the students will find attractive
- new staff and their experience
- special offers to tempt the students to attend.

You could link your special offers to any local or national health campaign, for example a colour run, Change4Life, walk 10,000 steps a day, the Paralympic Games or football World Cup.

Your team is going to design a poster to put up inside the sports centre and around your school to persuade them to come to the sports centre. In your group, work together to discuss the design for the poster. You should include:

- information about the new classes
- special offers
- cost
- opening times
- link to national or local campaign
- other ideas.

 **Remember**

A poster should be an attractive combination of words and pictures/photos. The purpose of a poster is usually to persuade people to buy or do something. All the information needed by the person looking at the poster must be included: for example a website address, a telephone number, a location or a date.

34

Speaking

 Fitness trends – now and then

In groups, you are going to compare modern fitness trends and behaviours with those of your parents or grandparents. Look at the seven pairs of fitness behaviours and decide in your group whether they are related to modern trends or trends from the past – there is one present and one past trend in each pair.

Keeping fit by going snowboarding
Keeping fit by doing aerobics

Getting excited about your Keep Fit class
Getting excited about your Cross Fit class

Wearing a tracksuit to go running
Wearing leggings and legwarmers to go jogging

Drinking a fizzy drink to rehydrate after exercising
Drinking water or a protein drink after exercising

Watching a workout video on the television
Watching a zumba video on YouTube

Hula hooping to stay fit
Kite surfing to stay fit

Wearing sweatbands around your wrists
Wearing a fitness tracker or smart watch on your wrist

Now discuss in your groups if you would you like to try some past fitness trends or if you prefer the modern trends. While you are talking, always check that you understand what other members of the group are saying. You can do this by asking questions to check what someone has said using phrases such as: 'Do you mean that …' and 'Are you saying that …'.

Reading corner

 Reading corner: Factual novel
Breaking the Jump

Read the following extract from *Breaking the Jump* by Julie Angel, a factual novel about parkour (also called freerunning), a fitness trend where people use structures like buildings and fences to move around.

By the time I started filming the London Parkour **scene** in 2004, I still **considered myself 'sporty'**. The truth was I hadn't done any kind of real exercise for ten years. What's more, I hadn't missed it. But as I watched members of the **Urban** Freeflow team training, it reminded me of the long-forgotten **thrill** of childhood adventures …

'Julie, you need to try this' said the little voice in my head which always starts **whispering** at me to do **ill-advised** things.

However, the voice of reason said something very different. There I was: a woman in her mid-thirties, with a successful career, … all my teeth, and few **noticeable scars**, perfectly happy with life. Beneath all my excuses for not trying Parkour I was terrified. I was scared in the usual sense of not wanting to fall and hurt myself …

The **discipline** was born in France but, like other **pioneering** French activities before it such as scuba diving and high-wire walking, it became popular internationally …

Not long after *Jump Britain* [a documentary about parkour] **aired** … the James Bond team had been inspired. They **tore up** the script for the original opening scene and rewrote it to **feature** the coolest thing anyone in the stunt world had seen for years. In 2006, [Sébastien Foucan, a famous freerunner] starred as the villain Mollaka in *Casino Royale* … and went on to appear in numerous commercials and music videos.

Understanding

Answer the following questions.

1. For how long did Julie not do proper exercise?
2. Give one example of something Sébastien Foucan appeared in after *Casino Royale*.
3. Did Julie consider herself to be athletic? How do you know?
4. Why does Julie say that she had 'all my teeth and few noticeable scars'?

Glossary

aired was shown on television

considered myself 'sporty' thought of myself as someone who was good at sport

discipline activity

feature include

ill-advised something it would be better not to do

noticeable scars obvious marks on the skin left by deep cuts that have healed

pioneering involving new ways of doing things

scene group

thrill excitement

tore up got rid of

urban to do with cities

whispering speaking very quietly

Writing workshop

Writing a factual story

You are going to write a factual story about the history of your favourite sport or fitness activity. A factual story is one based on fact that includes real people, places and events, but where the details of the events – for example conversations – might have been slightly altered.

Planning and research

First, you have to choose a sport or fitness activity to write about. Try and choose something you really enjoy participating in or watching, as this will make the writing even more enjoyable.

You will need to find out when your favourite sport or fitness activity first started and if there was a reason it started. Are there any well-known people who were involved early on? How did the sport or activity get its name? Was it named after a person, a place or something else?

You could also write about any major changes that have occurred since the sport or fitness activity was first introduced. Was there a single event that suddenly made it grow in popularity?

If you already do the sport or fitness activity and have a teacher or a coach, you could ask if they can help you. If you don't, try asking a local club for information about the history of the sport. If you have done this and still need more information, try researching the sport in your local or school library or on the Internet.

Writing, editing and proofreading

Now write your factual story. Remember, the facts you do include have to be accurate as you are writing a factual story not a fictional story. Write about 100 words.

Once you are finished, give it to your partner, who will proofread it for you. Tell your partner to look back at the Remember box on page 21 if they need a reminder of how to do this.

> **Remember**
>
> A factual story will use semi-formal language, so write in full sentences. Do not use slang, but you can use contractions such as 'don't' and you may want to use more informal vocabulary specific to the activity itself.

Progress assessment

Progress check

Answer the following questions.

1. Write a sentence to describe each of the following fitness trends.

   a yoga   **b** zumba   **c** colour running   (3 marks)

2. Give two reasons why you would like to take part in a colour run. (2 marks)

3. Choose the correct words or phrases from a–e to complete the following paragraph from Track 2.1.

   During the run you will have to go through …(a)… of colour, so don't wear your …(b)… clothes! Wear an old T-shirt and some …(c)… bottoms. Remember the photos from last year? The …(d)… ones were those where the runners wore white T-shirts because you could see all the colours …(e)….

a	streams	sports	showers
b	first	finest	fittest
c	colourful	jogging	runners
d	most sporty	most spectacular	most special
e	more clearly	cleaner	more cleanly

   (5 marks)

4. Choose the correct form of the adjective to fill the gaps in the following sentences.

   a I think yoga is the _____ kind of exercise. (better/best)

   b I was _____ that they raised so much money. (surprising/surprised) (2 marks)

5. In Track 2.2, when are the boys free to try a new fitness class? (1 mark)

6. Use the following words to write complete sentences.

   a perfectly/the/new/worked/app

   b the/all/wanted/luckily/to do/they/same class

   c definitely/booking/is/three places/Leo (3 marks)

7. Write a sentence to explain why your local sports centre should follow the latest fitness trends. (1 mark)

8. Why did Julie think she would not enjoy parkour at first? (1 mark)

9. Name two pioneering sports activities that began in France. (2 marks)

10. Write a paragraph to explain which fitness trend you would like to try and why. (5 marks)

(Total: 25 marks)

Progress assessment

Progress assessment

		😊	😐	😟
Reading skills	I can understand specific points in a text.	○	○	○
	I can use different reference resources to check meaning and learn more.	○	○	○
Use of English skills	I can use adjectives and ways to compare things.	○	○	○
	I can use adverbs in sentences and to compare things.	○	○	○
Listening skills	I can understand most of the specific points that someone is saying.	○	○	○
	I can understand most of the implied meaning when someone is speaking.	○	○	○
Speaking skills	I can check the main point of what someone else has said.	○	○	○
	I can explain my own point of view.	○	○	○
Writing skills	I can write, edit and proofread written work with some support.	○	○	○
	I can write with moderate grammatical accuracy.	○	○	○

✓ Action plan

Reading: I need to _____

Use of English: I need to _____

Listening: I need to _____

Speaking: I need to _____

Writing: I need to _____

I would like to know more about _____

3 Working abroad

Explore
- ideas about moving and working abroad
- ways to prepare for work

Create
- informal and formal emails
- a job application

Engage
- with a student
- with a doctor who works abroad

Collaborate
- to discuss moving to another country
- to talk about different ways to prepare for work

In this chapter you will:

Reflect
- on pronouns
- on prepositions

> The best prize that life has to offer is the chance to work hard at work worth doing.
> Theodore Roosevelt, US president 1901–09

> If you care about what you do and work hard at it, there isn't anything you can't do if you want to.
> Jim Henson, puppeteer

> One way to find success without working for it is to look it up in the dictionary.
> Stubby Currence, sports writer

Working abroad

Thinking ahead

1. What sort of job would you like to do in the future? Why?
2. Do you think you would like to work for yourself or for others? Why?
3. Would you like to work for a business or a charity? Explain your answer.

Word builder

Complete the sentences below with the correct words from the word box.

qualifications   salary   director   hard-working   branch

1. Ania wants to be a doctor so she hopes to get good _____.
2. Talia now works in a different _____ of the company.
3. Sanjay is the _____ of the charity and has 30 people working for him.
4. My mother has just had an increase in her _____.
5. It would be difficult to find someone who is more _____ than Jan.

Speaking about working abroad

Discuss the following questions in a small group.

1. Would you like to work abroad in the future? Explain why or why not.
2. How would you feel if you had to study or work abroad in the future? Would you be excited or nervous?
3. What would be the advantages and disadvantages of moving abroad to live or work?

Reading

📖 Ji-min's story

Read Ji-min's story below and then answer the questions that follow.

I am 15 years old and I have lived in different places because of my parents' work. For the first 14 years of my life, I lived in South Korea with my parents, my brother and my sister. Four years ago, we had to **pack up** and move to Seoul, the capital city, because my father got a **promotion** at work. He also earned a higher salary, so we moved into a bigger flat in the city centre.

My mother has good qualifications and is also very **hard-working**. Last year, she **was promoted** to become a director of the company she works for and she was asked to set up a new branch of the company in London. Our family moved again and now my parents work there and I go to school in London, too.

It was difficult at first. Although I had learned English before arriving here, speaking it to a friend in my classroom in Korea was not the same as speaking it to someone I did not know. However, I like languages and I was certain that my English would improve, which of course it has. I have spent much of my free time learning English. I have also told my mother that watching English television will help me understand both the language and the culture better – but I am not sure she agrees!

My brother is enjoying his new school and he loves playing football in the local youth team. My sister misses her friends back in Seoul but often talks to them using her tablet, which makes her feel better. I am really glad I have experienced living in different places because I think it will help me find a job more easily in the future.

Understanding

A Choose the correct answer to each of the following questions.

1. For how many years did Ji-min live in South Korea?
   - **a** four
   - **b** fourteen
   - **c** fifteen

Glossary

hard-working putting a lot of effort into a job

pack up to collect all your things together

promotion a more important job

was promoted was offered a better job

Reading

2. Why were Ji-min's family able to move into a bigger flat in Seoul?
   a because Seoul is a capital city
   b because the flat was in the city centre
   c because her father earned more money

3. What might Ji-min's mother say if Ji-min says that watching television will improve her English?
   a "That sounds like a fantastic idea – television will improve your English."
   b "I am not convinced that television will improve your English."
   c "That sounds like a bad idea – television will definitely not improve your English."

B Answer these questions.

1. Why do you think Ji-min's mother got a promotion? Suggest two reasons.
2. Was Ji-min happy about moving for her parents' work? How do you know?
3. How do you think her brother and sister felt? Explain your answer.

C Answer these questions.

1. How can we best prepare to move to a different country or a different part of our own country? Write one sentence to give advice to someone about to move away.
2. If you move to a new area, you may feel different emotions. Write down four adjectives to describe how you would feel if you had to move because a family member changed their job.

Writing an informal email

Imagine you have moved with your family to another part of the country or have moved abroad. Write an informal email to one of your friends who you have left behind. In your email:
- describe the house or flat you are now living in
- say what your new school is like
- explain how you feel about the move.

Write about 100 words.

Challenge

Write down four advantages of moving abroad for work (or study if your family is moving abroad for work). Create an advertisement to persuade people from another place to come to your town or area for work. Include the four advantages you have listed. You can do this by using them as quotations from local people, as well as including a picture of the area.

Use of English

Demonstrative and indefinite pronouns

We use **demonstrative pronouns** ('this', 'these', 'that' and 'those') to talk about a particular person, thing or idea.

Examples: **This** is my friend, Zak.   Are you happy with **that**?
These are my books.   Are **those** your shoes?

To be less specific, we can use **indefinite pronouns**. We use pronouns ending in –body or –one (somebody, anybody, everyone, etc.) to talk about people. Pronouns ending in –thing (something, anything, everything) refer to things and pronouns ending in 'where' (somewhere, anywhere, everywhere) refer to places.

Examples: **Everyone** has arrived.   He hasn't eaten **anything**.   She found **somewhere** to stay.

We can also use indefinite pronouns to talk about amounts or quantities (some, any, more, many, less, much, none etc.).

Examples: I have come without my money. Please will you you lend me **some**?

Using demonstrative and indefinite pronouns

A Fill the gaps in the following sentences with a suitable demonstrative pronoun. More than one answer may be possible.

1. _____ are very good ideas!
2. Come in. _____ is where I work.
3. I really enjoyed reading _____. It was an interesting story.
4. _____ are my sisters, Eva and Sofia.

B Fill in the gaps in the following conversation with pronouns from the word box.

| anyone | this | something | that |
| much | everyone | somewhere | someone |

Adel: Have you seen _____? It's an advertisement for a job in Madrid. Why don't you apply?

Nada: Yes, _____ at work showed me _____ yesterday. I would love to do _____ in a different country for a while. And _____ hot and sunny would be good.

Adel: I don't know _____ about Madrid. Do you know _____ who lives there?

Nada: No, but I'm sure _____ is very friendly.

Remember

- We usually use 'this' and 'these' for people and things that are near to us and 'that' and 'those' for people and things that are not near.

- Many pronouns can also be used as determiners. Determiners come before nouns (see page 10).

44

Use of English

Reflexive pronouns

The reflexive pronouns are:

singular	myself, yourself, herself, himself, itself
plural	ourselves, yourselves, themselves

We use reflexive pronouns when the subject and object of a verb are the same person or thing.

Example: She is teaching **herself** to speak English.

We also use reflexive pronouns to emphasise (give importance to) the person or thing we are talking about.

Example: The director **herself** interviewed me for the job.

We can use reflexive pronouns with 'by' to mean 'alone', 'on your own' or 'without help'.

Example: Did you live there **by yourself**?

Using reflexive pronouns

A Use the correct reflexive pronouns to complete the following sentences.

1. When we arrived, we introduced _____ to the manager.
2. It wasn't your fault. You shouldn't blame _____.
3. The employees _____ decide when to take their breaks.
4. My sister really enjoyed _____ at school today.
5. I'll write _____ a note so I won't forget to call you.

B Rewrite the following sentences using reflexive pronouns with 'by'. The first one has been done for you.

1. He ate his lunch alone.
   He ate his lunch by himself.
2. Was she sitting on her own?
3. If you get a job abroad, do you think you will live alone?
4. I fixed the computer without any help.

C Write four sentences of your own using reflexive pronouns of your choice.

Remember

- When we do something for ourselves, we often use verb + reflexive pronoun + object.

  Example: I made myself some lunch.

- We often use reflexive pronouns after 'enjoy', 'behave' and 'help'.

  Example: Help yourself to a glass of water.

Listening

Living and working abroad

Word builder

Match the word or phrase on the left with the definition on the right.

visa	pieces of paper with official information on them
homesick	a mark on your passport that means you can enter a certain country
documents	the money used in a particular country
currency	a feeling of missing friends and family

Track 3.1: Living and working abroad

You are going to hear Silas talking about moving to a different country for work and how he prepared himself to move from one country to another. Listen to his talk and then answer the questions.

Understanding

A Choose the correct answer to each of the following questions.

1. How long did Silas live in the UK for?
   - **a** three months
   - **b** three years
   - **c** eight years
2. Which country is Silas working in now?
   - **a** Nambia
   - **b** Malawi
   - **c** New Zealand
3. Why do you need a visa?
   - **a** It allows you to enter a particular country.
   - **b** It gives you good qualifications.
   - **c** It gets you a good job in another country.
4. How much local currency does Silas think you should take abroad?
   - **a** none
   - **b** a little
   - **c** a lot
5. What is his reason for saying this?
   - **a** You might spend it too quickly.
   - **b** It is easier to get currency after you arrive.
   - **c** It might get lost.

Glossary
work permit a document that allows you to work in a certain country

Listening

B Answer these questions.

1. Why might you choose to live in the capital city if you were studying or working abroad?
2. Silas says about packing: "Put everything out you would like to take and then take half away!" What does he mean by this?
3. How does Silas describe working in another country?

C Answer these questions.

1. Name two possible problems when going to study or work in another country.
2. Name two benefits of going to study or work in another country.

> **Challenge**
>
> Has anyone in your school moved from a different country, area or town? Perhaps one of the students has moved to study at your school, or one of the teachers may have moved there. Find someone who came from a different place and ask them what they think of your school and why they are pleased to have moved. When you have completed your research, report back to the class.

💬 Speaking: What do you think?

You are going to talk about moving to another country for work or for study.

1. In pairs, tell each other which country you would most like to travel to, either for work or for study. Give at least two reasons for your choice.
2. In the recording, Silas said that you can't take everything you would like to with you. What would you find hardest to leave behind? Tell each other in groups and give a reason for your choice.

✏️ Writing a formal email

Write a short formal email to Silas thanking him for his talk. Tell him which part of his talk you found most useful for someone thinking of moving abroad to work. Write 60–80 words.

> **Remember**
>
> Remember to use formal language in your email and check your spelling, grammar and punctuation carefully.

Use of English

Prepositions

We use prepositions to show the relationship between words in a sentence. Prepositions are usually followed by a noun, a noun phrase or a pronoun.

We can use prepositions to talk about:

- **location** or **place** (where something is)

    Examples: **in** the office, **at** the bus stop, **on** the round table, **above** the door, **on top of** the tall cupboard, **next to** me, **outside** the city, **near/close to** the river, **in front of** the building, **opposite** the cinema, **between** the two chairs, **among** the books

- **time** (when something happens, or for how long)

    Examples: **at** the weekend, **at** 6 o'clock, **in** the morning, **in** 2016, **in** ten minutes, **on** Tuesday, **by** next week, **for** five hours, **during** the night, **since** 2010, **after** work

- **movement** or **direction**

    Examples: **to** the shop, **into** the house, **out of** the building, **onto** the bus, **off** the train, **along** the path, **past** the house, **through** the gate, **across** the bridge, **over** the wall

Using prepositions

A Use a suitable preposition to fill the gaps in the following sentences.

1. I'll be back _____ about two hours. I caught the wrong train _____ mistake.
2. I was waiting _____ the bus stop _____ an hour this morning.
3. I saw you running _____ work. Did you arrive _____ time?
4. Sara's not _____ work this week. She's _____ holiday.

B Rewrite the following paragraph underlining all the prepositions.

Silas has lived in the city centre since 2015, when he moved to Wellington. His house is opposite the train station. He just needs to walk across the road, get on a train, and he can be at the airport in about 20 minutes. His office is close to the harbour. At weekends during the summer, he often cycles out of the city.

C Write three sentences of your own using the phrases 'by chance', 'on purpose' and 'in advance'.

Remember

We often use prepositions before nouns in phrases such as: at school, at last, by chance, by mistake, in time, in advance, on purpose, on time, on the phone, on holiday.

Challenge

Write three headings 'Place', 'Time' and 'Movement'. Decide how each of the prepositions in exercise B is used and then write the prepositions under the right headings.

48

Use of English

More prepositions

We often use prepositions after adjectives, nouns and verbs. Look at these examples.

Adjective + preposition

at	for	of	about	with
good at, bad at	good for, qualified for	afraid of, tired of	angry about, excited about	pleased with, disappointed with

Noun + preposition

to	for	with	in	on
solution to, reply to	room for, reason for	meeting with, discussion with	delay in, expert in	advice on, talk on

Verb + preposition

on	with	for	in	of
insist on, concentrate on	agree with, deal with	apply for, prepare for	succeed in, believe in	approve of, dream of

Using prepositions

A Complete the sentences using prepositions from the box.

> in   at   for

1. Silas soon became better _____ English.
2. What was his reason _____ going to London?
3. Silas believes _____ working hard and having fun.

B Fill the gaps in the following email with a noun, adjective, verb or preposition from the box.

> to   on   for
> room   succeed   prepare   about

Hi Silas

I listened _____ your talk _____ living and working abroad today. I recently applied _____ a job in Nepal. If I _____ in getting the job, I will soon have to _____ for my move! I am a bit worried _____ having too much luggage! Should I find _____ for things that remind me of home?

Lucia

Remember

When a verb follows a preposition, we use the –ing form of the verb.

Challenge

Write three sentences of your own using a preposition after a noun, adjective and verb of your choice.

Speaking

Living and working abroad

Word builder

Use a word from the word box to complete the sentences that follow.

| opportunity | qualities | professional |

1. Kay was very _____ in the way she did her job.
2. My cousin has applied for a job abroad – it seems like a wonderful _____.
3. Omar has great personal _____, so he is really good with customers.

Living and working abroad

You are going to give a talk to your classmates about travelling from your country to another country of your choice. Tell them:

- why you chose that country
- what you intend to take with you
- what cultural differences there might be and how will you prepare for them.

You should also end your talk by saying why you have the qualities needed to work abroad in the future. First, decide on two qualities that are needed and then explain why you have them. Try to use some of vocabulary you have learned in the unit so far.

Speaking

💬 Preparing for work

There are several things you can do to prepare for working in the future. Many people start by going to school and, if they can, then go to college or university. If they can't or choose not to, they might join a company as an apprentice. This means they learn the skills they need to do a certain job so they can do that job for a higher salary in the future.

Tell your partner if you think you will study more when you leave school, or become an apprentice, find a job or maybe work during the day and study in the evenings. What would be the advantages of your choice? What would be the disadvantages?

Some people might work for one person, for a large company or choose to start their own business. They might stay in the same town, travel to a different part of the country, or move abroad.

Tell your partner if you think you will stay in your home town, move to a different part of the country or move abroad when you start work.

What do you think you will do between now and having your first job? How will you get that first job?

With your partner, explain your plan and why you have decided to do it. For example, if you want to become a doctor, you would need to finish school and then go to medical school at university.

Reading corner

📖 Reading corner: Working abroad

Magda has spent the last two years working abroad. Read the article from a newspaper based on an interview she gave a journalist about her time working in a different country.

I spent the day talking to Magda Kurka. She has spent the last two years working here in Singapore.

Magda was born in Czestochowa, in Poland. After she left school, she went to Krakow to go to university. She had studied science at school and enjoyed it very much; she particularly liked biology as she had an enthusiastic biology teacher. She decided to study medicine at university so she could become a doctor. At the same time, she had language lessons to improve her English because she knew she wanted to travel and that English would be useful for her when talking to other people around the world.

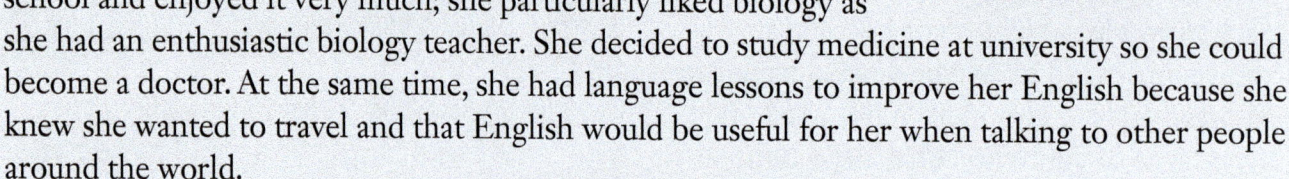

I wanted to know why Magda had become a doctor and she told me that being a doctor had always been her **dream job**; ever since she was a child, she had wanted to help people and knew that was what she wanted to do in the future.

So why did she choose to come to Singapore? Magda said it was because she had seen a documentary about Singapore when she was a teenager and had decided then that she would come and live in Singapore at some point. Her favourite part of Singapore is the waterfalls in the botanic gardens – good choice!

I asked Magda what she had learned by being in a different country and she said that it was exciting to learn about a different culture, and that the winters were definitely warmer than in Poland! Finally, I asked Magda what advice she would give someone thinking about working in a different country. She said people should just apply for the job and be ready to learn a lot about the country before they moved there. She said that even though she had read about Singapore before coming here, she has since learned things that she would never have read about in a guidebook or on the Internet and that is what is so exciting about working abroad.

Understanding

Answer the following questions.

1. What subjects did Magda enjoy at school? Why do you think this was?
2. Why did Magda want to go to Singapore?
3. What does the writer think about Magda's favourite part of Singapore?
4. Does Magda think it is better to travel to a country if you want to learn about it? Explain your answer.

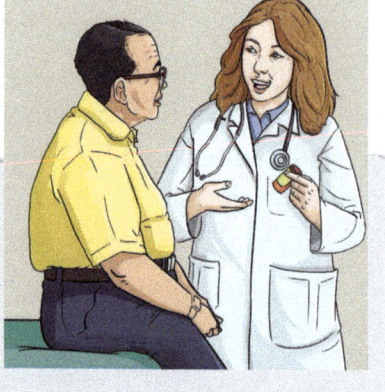

Glossary

dream job the job someone would most like to do

Writing workshop

Writing an application for your dream job

Planning and writing

What job would you like in the future and which country would you most like to work in?

You are going to write a letter to a company of your choice to apply for your dream future job. You can do the job in any country you choose.

Before you start, write brief notes to answer the following questions:

- What is your dream job?
- Which company do you want to work for?
- Which country do you want to work in?

When writing your letter, remember to explain why you are suitable for the job – think about you as a person, your qualifications and your attitude to work. Your letter should be about 150–200 words long.

Remember

Remember to use the correct layout for a formal letter and to use formal language.

Checking spelling, grammar and punctuation

When you have written your letter, check your spelling, grammar and punctuation carefully. Then give it to a partner so they can check that you have used the correct layout and that you have used formal language. They should also check your spelling, grammar and punctuation and correct any mistakes you have made.

Progress assessment

Progress check

Answer the following questions.

1. 'One way to find success without working for it is to look it up in the dictionary.'
   Explain what this quotation means in your own words. (1 mark)

2. Name two things that Ji-min's brother likes about London. (2 marks)

3. Complete the following sentences with the correct pronoun from the brackets.
   a Have you heard _____ about your promotion? (anyone/anything/everything)
   b _____ are my books. (This/That/These)
   c Did you go travelling by _____? (you/himself/yourself)
   d The manager _____ interviewed me. (itself/herself/myself) (4 marks)

4. Name four countries Silas has lived in. (4 marks)

5. Which of the following are official documents that someone might need to work abroad? Choose all the correct answers.
   a visa   b passport   c dictionary   d work permit   (3 marks)

6. What piece of advice would you give to someone thinking about working abroad? (1 mark)

7. Fill the gaps in the following sentences with a suitable preposition.
   a Ola wants to get a job _____ the local building firm.
   b He cycles _____ a bridge to get to work.
   c He found a very good solution _____ the problem. (3 marks)

8. Complete the sentences using each of the words in the box.

   professional   qualifications   promoted

   Martin has excellent _____ and a really _____ attitude to his job.
   It is likely that he will be _____ to manager soon. (3 marks)

9. Going to school is one way you can prepare for working in the future. Name one other way. (1 mark)

10. Which job would give you the greatest opportunities for travel? Explain your answer. (3 marks)

(Total: 25 marks)

Progress assessment

		😊	😕	🙁
Reading skills	I can understand implied meaning in texts.	○	○	○
	I can work out meaning from the context.	○	○	○
	I can recognise typical features in written texts.	○	○	○
Use of English skills	I can use different types of pronouns.	○	○	○
	I can use prepositions before nouns, adjectives and verbs.	○	○	○
Listening skills	I can work out meaning from the context.	○	○	○
Speaking skills	I can explain my own point of view.	○	○	○
	I can explain advantages and disadvantages of ideas, plans and arrangements.	○	○	○
Writing skills	I can write with moderate grammatical accuracy.	○	○	○
	I can use the correct style, register and layout.	○	○	○
	I can use correct punctuation and spelling.	○	○	○

Action plan

Reading: I need to _____

Use of English: I need to _____

Listening: I need to _____

Speaking: I need to _____

Writing: I need to _____

I would like to know more about _____

4 Arts and crafts

Explore
- how to weave a paper basket
- different kinds of arts and crafts

Create
- a speech
- a biography

Engage
- with an entrepreneur
- with an artist

Collaborate
- to discuss ideas
- to make a group presentation

In this chapter you will:

Reflect
- on active and passive forms
- on the present and past continuous

Art is as natural as sunshine and as vital as nourishment. MaryAnn F. Kohl, author of art books for children

Art takes nature as its model. Aristotle, ancient Greek philosopher

Creativity is intelligence having fun. Albert Einstein, scientist

Arts and crafts

Thinking ahead

1. How many different kinds of arts and crafts can you think of?
2. Why do you think people enjoy doing arts and crafts?
3. What are the advantages of learning an art or craft?

Word builder

Look at the notice about different craft courses available at a local college. Rewrite the sentences, filling the gaps with the correct words from the word box.

textiles	jewellery	crafts	sculpture
creative	hobby	weave	relaxation

Calling all crafters!

Do you do any arts or _____?

Would you like to try out a new _____?

Are you in need of some _____ or do you just want to be _____?

Come and enrol on a course at New College on Monday 15 September at 7 p.m.

You can learn how to sew _____, make a _____, design your own _____ or even _____ a basket.

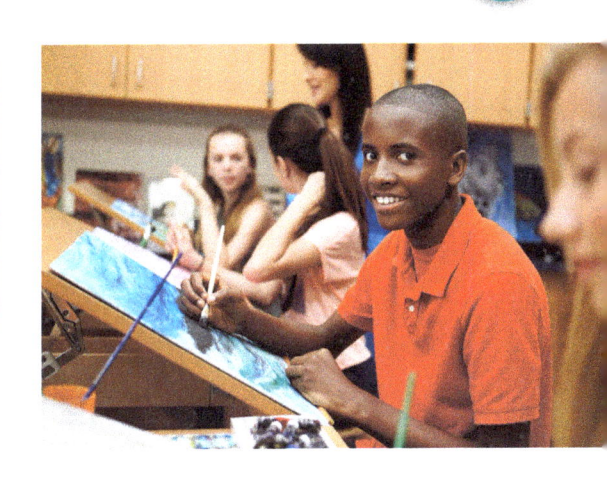

Speaking about arts and crafts

Discuss the following questions with a partner. See how many words you can use from the Word builder.

1. Can you think of an art or craft that was not included in the Word builder?
2. Which art or craft would you most like to do?
3. Do you think it is important to have a hobby? Explain your answer.

Reading

📖 Paper basket weaving

Read the instructions below, which explain how to weave a basket out of paper.

Glossary

bend make a curve in something
cardboard strong paper board
glue a substance used to stick things together
narrower smaller in width
protection something to stop damage
upright something that is standing up, in this case a vertical tube

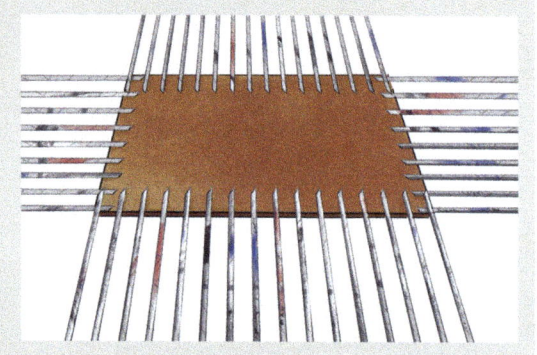

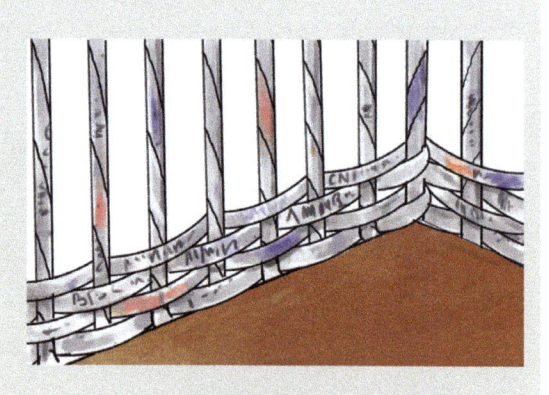

How to weave a paper basket

Time needed: 4 hours

Paper weaving can be great for relaxation and a fantastic way to be creative.

Step 1: Preparation

First, cut long pieces of newspaper that are about 10 cm wide and then roll them into thin tubes. Keep each tube together by sticking it with **glue**.

Cut two rectangular pieces of **cardboard** and stick double-sided tape around the edges. Stick the paper tubes to the tape around the sides of one piece of cardboard.

Use glue to stick the second piece of cardboard on top of the cardboard with tubes. Place a heavy book on top and leave to dry. You can cover the top layer with any material you like.

Step 2: Weaving the basket

To start weaving, join two tubes and then **bend** in half and make them go in and out around the first **upright**. Then continue to weave in and out of the uprights, making sure the paper tubes are tight while you are weaving. When you reach the corners, do an extra turn.

Step 3: How to make long tubes

As you reach the end of a tube, take a new tube and put the **narrower** end into the end of the tube you are using. As you weave each row, it's easy to make the paper tubes longer as you work.

Continue to add rows until you reach the height of basket you want.

To finish, bend the tubes over and push them down through the weave on the inside. Then paint your basket. This provides **protection** for the newspaper and also makes it stronger.

Be creative, weave different designs!

Reading

Understanding

A Answer the following questions.

1. What is the purpose of the instructions on page 58? Choose the correct answer.
   a to give information about how to weave a paper basket
   b to encourage people to start a new hobby
   c to persuade people to join a weaving class
2. How long might it take to weave a paper basket?

B Answer the following questions.

1. Why might someone decide to take up paper weaving? List two reasons.
2. Why is it important to paint the basket when you have finished? Choose the correct answer.
   a to make it look attractive
   b to glue the paper together and protect the paper
   c to protect the paper and make it stronger

C List three ways you could be creative with basket weaving.

Speaking: Role play

Imagine that you have joined a new arts and crafts class, such as paper weaving. Talk to a partner, in a role play, about what you did and what you enjoyed doing. Try and use vocabulary you have learned from the unit so far. Persuade your friend to join the class too. Think about the words and phrases you will use to encourage your friend to join you in your new class.

Writing a formal letter

Imagine you have woven a paper basket and you are going to enter a competition called 'Ways to be Creative'. Write a formal letter to Mr Choudry, the competition organiser, explaining what you did and how you have been creative. Write 40–60 words.

Remember

In a formal letter, you need to remember the following:
- 'Dear Mr, Mrs or Ms' ends with 'Yours sincerely'
- 'Dear Sir or Madam' ends with 'Yours faithfully'

Use of English

Active and passive forms

We use **active** verbs to say what the subject of a sentence does.

Examples: The school **holds** lots of classes.   Mara **chose** a class.

We use **passive** verbs to say what the subject of the verb has done to it. We can use 'by' + person to say who did the action.

Examples: Lots of classes **are held by** the school.   A class **was chosen by** Mara.

We do not always use 'by' + person in passive sentences. Often, the 'doer' of the action (the agent) is not known, not important or obvious.

Example: The students' paintings were displayed at the end of term.

We often use 'it' with the passive form of verbs such as 'say', 'decide', 'feel' and 'think' followed by 'that'.

Examples: **It is said that** New College is one of the best places to learn arts and crafts.

It was felt that the class was too difficult.

Using active and passive forms

A For each number in the paragraph below, choose the correct verb form from the list.

In the past, people often …(1)… food in handmade baskets. The baskets …(2)… made from natural materials such as grass. In ancient times, the finest baskets were …(3)… so tightly that they could hold water. Today, basket-making …(4)… still …(5)… in many countries around the world.

1. was stored   stores   store   stored
2. was   were   are   is
3. weaving   weaved   woven   weaves
4. was   are   is   were
5. practising   practise   practising practised

Remember

To make a passive verb, we use a form of the verb 'be' with a past participle. To change the tense, we change the form of 'be'.

Examples:

Jewellery-making classes are held on Tuesdays. Last term, jewellery-making classes were held on Wednesdays.

B Change the following sentences into the passive. Remember to use the right tense and decide whether to include 'by' and the agent.

1. New College offers all kinds of arts and crafts courses.
2. They cancelled the sewing class last week.
3. People believe that basket-making is one of the oldest crafts in the world.

Use of English

Causative forms

When we arrange for someone to do something for us, we often use the causative form **have something done**. In informal English, we often use **get something done**.

Examples: The college **has its windows cleaned** every month.
Someone needs to **get this broken window mended**.

We can use causative forms in negative sentences and questions. In the present simple, we use 'do/does/don't/doesn't' with 'have/get'. In the past simple, we use 'did/didn't' with 'have/get'.

Examples: **Do** you **have** your teeth checked regularly?
He **doesn't have** his eyes tested very often.
Where **did** you **get** your hair cut?
Didn't you **have** your car repaired yesterday?

We can also use 'have/get something done' when something bad or unpleasant happens. In this case, the subject is affected by an action that they did not cause.

Example: I **had my purse stolen** yesterday.

Using causative forms

A Use the correct form of 'have' or 'get' and the verb in brackets to complete these sentences.

1. The school _____ some new cupboards _____ in the art room last term. (fit)
2. The college _____ new art supplies _____ at the beginning of every term. (deliver)
3. They _____ the old windows _____ tomorrow. (replace)

B Complete the second sentence so that it means the same as the first, using the word in brackets and any other words you need. Do not change the word given. The first one has been done for you.

1. Was your car repaired yesterday? (get)
   Did you *get your car repaired yesterday?*
2. Some of the school's buildings were damaged in the storm. (had)
   The school _____.
3. When were your teeth last checked by a dentist? (did)
   When _____?
4. The school's windows weren't cleaned last month. (didn't)
   The school _____.

Remember

- To use causative forms with 'have' or 'get', we use: subject + a form of 'have/get' + object + past participle.
- We can use causative forms in any tense. To change the tense, we change the form of 'have' or 'get'.

Examples: He had his portrait painted by a professional artist. I am getting my computer fixed tomorrow.

61

Listening

My hobby became my business

Track 4.1: My hobby became my business

You are going to listen to Fivi, an entrepreneur, explaining how she made her hobby into her business. Listen to the recording and answer the questions.

"How my hobby became my my business"

Glossary

invest put money into something, for example a business

recommend put forward

savings money that someone has saved

unique different and special

word spread more and more people told each other about it

Understanding

A Choose the correct answer to each of the following questions.

1. What does 'Jewellery for Me' do?
   a craft and change jewellery
   b repair jewellery
   c craft and design jewellery

2. How does Fivi find her materials for making jewellery?
   a from markets and shops
   b from markets and online websites
   c from websites and shops

3. Where did Fivi get the money from to buy her materials?
   a She had savings.
   b She got a loan from the bank.
   c She borrowed from friends and family.

4. Who were Fivi's first customers?
   a people from Australia
   b customers from her website
   c friends and family

Listening

B Answer the following questions.

1. For each letter in brackets, choose the correct word from the box below.

   Fivi: I am …(a)… a special necklace for a customer today.

   Colleague: What …(b)… do you need?

   Fivi: The customer asked for white, natural-looking jewellery, so I will use …(c)….

   Colleague: Would you like me to …(d)… an address label?

   Fivi: That's a good idea, but first can you help me make some …(e)… earrings, as they need to match the necklace?

a	designing	painting	drawing
b	materials	paper	pen
c	plastic	ruby	pearls
d	weave	sew	print
e	stone	pearl	basket

2. Which of the following statements might Fivi Stavrou say about making your hobby your career?
   - a "It is really hard work and I regret it."
   - b "It was the best thing I have ever done in my life."
   - c "It has good and bad points."

C Answer the following questions.

1. What materials does Fivi use in her jewellery design? Choose the correct answer.
   - a gold and silver
   - b simple and unusual
   - c expensive and daring

2. Fivi is described as an entrepreneur. What do you think the word 'entrepreneur' means?

3. Write down three things Fivi enjoys about her new career.

✏️ Writing about Fivi's opinion

What is Fivi's opinion of making a hobby your career? Write one paragraph to summarise this.

When you have finished, share your paragraph with a partner. Do you agree?

Use of English

The present continuous

We make the present continuous with a present form of 'be' (am/is/are) + a present participle (–ing). We use the present continuous to talk about:

- actions that are happening at or around the time we are speaking, or situations that are temporary

    Examples: I **am waiting** for my friend.
    I **am reading** a good book.
    I **am looking** after my friend's house while she is away.

- situations that are changing at the present time

    Example: A lot of new shops **are opening** in this area.

- with 'always' to talk about things that happen again and again and things we find annoying

    Examples: It**'s always raining**!
    She **is always borrowing** my phone!

- actions that are planned for the future.

    Example: My uncle **is arriving** on Sunday.

> **Remember**
>
> - To make a passive present continuous form, we use a present form of 'be' + being + past participle.
>
>   *Example*: They are mending my necklace.
>   → My necklace is being mended.
>
> - To make a question form using the present continuous, we put the auxiliary (am/is/are) before the subject.
>
>   *Examples*: Are you eating your lunch? What is she doing?

Using the present continuous

A Rewrite these sentences in the present continuous.

1. Fivi feels very happy at the moment.
2. She travels all over the world.
3. Her business grows bigger every month.
4. This customer always changes her mind!

B Complete these sentences using the present continuous form of the verbs in brackets.

1. She _____ to find some unusual materials. (try)
2. What _____ she _____? (make)
3. _____ she _____ of opening some shops? (think)

C Rewrite the following sentences using passive forms of the present continuous.

1. People in many different countries are wearing her jewellery.
2. She is designing this bracelet for someone in Australia.
3. Her business is receiving more orders every week.

64

Use of English

The past continuous

To make the past continuous we use a past form of 'be' (was/were) + a present participle. We use the past continuous to talk about:

- something that was happening over a period of time or at a particular time in the past

  Examples: I **wasn't feeling** well yesterday. What **were** you **doing** at 10 o'clock this morning?

- temporary or changing situations in the past

  Examples: **Were** you **living** in Australia last year? She **was getting** more orders every week.

- annoying situations in the past, often with 'always'

  Example: They **were always arguing**.

- actions in the past that were interrupted by another action.

  Example: I **was waiting** for a bus when it started to rain.

We also use the past continuous to give background information or a setting for a story.

  Example: The sun **was shining** and the birds **were singing**.

Using the past continuous

A Fill the gaps with past continuous forms of the verbs in brackets.

1. What _____ you _____ in Germany last year? (do)
2. She _____ on her computer when she had a good idea. (work)
3. He _____ always _____ late for school. (arrive)
4. She _____ more orders every week. (get)

B Rewrite the following sentences in the past continuous.

1. Aren't you listening to what she is saying?
2. I didn't enjoy my job and I felt very tired.
3. It started to snow and it got dark.

C Rewrite the following sentences using passive forms of the past continuous.

1. She was making the bracelet out of feathers and leather.
2. They were showing the film earlier this evening.
3. Was the teacher collecting the books?

Remember

To make a passive past continuous form, we use a past form of 'be' + being + past participle.

Example: The customer was checking the design. ⟶ The design was being checked by the customer.

Speaking

💬 Different arts and crafts

Look at the pictures of people doing different art and craft activities. Match each picture with one of the activities from the word box.

| glass painting | painting | quilting | pottery |

💬 Discussing arts and crafts

With a partner, take turns to talk about each of the following questions. Then share your ideas with another pair.

1. What is each person making or doing in the photograph or picture? Use the present continuous in your answers and try to use powerful adjectives or adverbs to describe the activity.
2. What are the advantages and disadvantages of learning a new art or craft at school rather than at home?
3. Do you think you could make a business from any of these activities? If so, how?

Speaking

Word builder

Match the words and phrases on the left with the correct meanings on the right.

textiles	making a cover from different pieces of cloth
knitting	types of cloth
embroidery	making a picture out of different materials
glass blowing	making objects out of glass by blowing
collage	using a needle in a decorative way
quilting	stitching wool together to make items

Speaking: Group presentation

In a small group, prepare a presentation to persuade your school to introduce a new arts and crafts subject. Everybody in the group must take part. Use words from the Word builder to help you. Your class will then vote on the best idea.

You will need to include in your presentation:

- an introduction – what your arts/crafts subject is
- why your subject should be chosen (What advantages does it have over other subjects?)
- language to persuade.

67

Reading corner

📖 Reading corner: *Artist*

Chinwe Roy was born in Nigeria and moved to the UK in 1975. She always wanted to be an artist – even from childhood – and achieved her dream. Read the following extract from the first chapter of Verna Wilkins' biography of Chinwe Roy, *Artist*.

Dreams

Even as a five year old girl in Primary School, Chinwe didn't like Maths. She wanted to draw and paint pictures…

"Work harder or else!" warned her class teacher. So, in Maths lessons, Chinwe put her head down and worked **furiously,** glancing up at the teacher every minute or two.

Then, one day, his eyes narrowed and he **bellowed,** "Come here Chinwe. Immediately. Bring your work with you." Chinwe froze.

The teacher strode over to her desk. "What's this?" he shouted, staring at a crazy cartoon of his own head, huge on a **shrunken** body…

For the entire hour of her next Maths lesson, the teacher made her stand on top of her desk. Her humiliation was complete.

Chinwe lost her heart and worked her way to the bottom of her class…

Many years later, in the year 2000, far beyond her early dreams, and thousands of kilometres away from her African classroom, Chinwe was chosen to do a **portrait** of Her Majesty, Queen Elizabeth II, the most **prestigious** job in the world of portrait painting. Chinwe Roy was the first black person ever to paint the Queen.

Understanding

Answer the following questions.

1. What did Chinwe want to do more than Maths?
2. Why did Chinwe have to stand on top of her desk?
3. Why didn't Chinwe do well at school?
4. Which phrase tells us that Chinwe didn't do well in school?

Glossary

bellowed shouted loudly

furiously angrily

portrait a painting or drawing of somebody

prestigious respected and admired

shrunken smaller in size

Writing workshop

✏️ Writing a biography

You are going to plan and write a short biography of an artist of your choice.

Planning

As a class, brainstorm different artists you might like to choose.

When you have chosen your artist, find out as much as you can about them. You might like to use a spider diagram to organise your ideas. You should research:

- when and where the artist was born (and perhaps other details about their childhood)
- what kind of art they are famous for
- names or examples of their work.

Drafting

Now use the checklist below to help you draft your biography. Then work with a partner to check each other's drafts. Say what you found interesting in your partner's biography and make one suggestion as to how it could be even better.

Checklist

- Introduction – who the person is and why you have chosen them
- Paragraph 2 – the past: background information
- Paragraph 3 – the present: why they are famous and what they have achieved
- Paragraph 4 – the future: if the artist is still alive, do they have future projects?; if the artist is not alive, has their work influenced artists today?
- Conclusion – what has this artist brought to the world?

Writing, editing and proofreading

Now write your biography. Write 150–200 words. Then read it through carefully and correct any mistakes you can find.

📖 Suggested reading

If you enjoyed reading the extract on page 68, you could read the whole book and then read another biography, such as *Who was Walt Disney?* by Whitney Stewart or *Who was Leonardo Da Vinci?* by Roberta Edwards.

💡 Remember

Biographies are:
- written in the third person
- usually in the past tense
- often in chronological (time) order and include dates.

Progress check

Answer the following questions.

1. Write two adjectives to describe the hobby of paper weaving. (2 marks)

2. What do you use to stop the paper rolls coming apart? Choose the correct answer.
   - a glue
   - b double-sided tape (1 mark)

3. Change the following sentences into the passive.
   - a They gave Sara a place on the glass-making course.
   - b People say that basket-making is one of the oldest crafts.
   - c They replaced the art teacher last term. (3 marks)

4. Rewrite the following sentences using the causative form 'have/get something done'.
   - a Her portrait was painted by a well-known artist.
   - b Someone stole my phone yesterday. (2 marks)

5. How much money did Fivi have when she first started her business? Choose the correct answer.
   - a £300
   - b £3000
   - c £30,000 (1 mark)

6. Do you think it is a good idea to turn a hobby into a business? Give a reason for your answer. (2 marks)

7. Rewrite the following sentences using present or past continuous forms of the verbs in brackets.
   - a She _____ (enjoy) her work at the moment and her business _____ (grow).
   - b Last week, she _____ (work) on the design for a bracelet and next week she _____ (visit) Japan. (4 marks)

8. How did Chinwe feel when her teacher 'bellowed' at her? What phrase tells us this? (2 marks)

9. Name three things that show that *Artist* is an example of a biography. (3 marks)

10. What would you say to Chinwe if you had met her when she was five years old? Write a paragraph to explain your answer. (5 marks)

(Total: 25 marks)

Progress assessment

Progress assessment

		😊	😕	🙁
Reading skills	I can understand specific points in a text.	○	○	○
	I can recognise typical features in written texts.	○	○	○
	I can read a growing range of non-fiction texts.	○	○	○
Use of English skills	I can use active and passive past and present simple forms, including causative forms.	○	○	○
	I can use the present and past continuous, including some passive forms.	○	○	○
Listening skills	I can understand most of the specific points that someone is saying.	○	○	○
	I can recognise what someone's opinion is when they are speaking.	○	○	○
Speaking skills	I can use a growing range of subject-specific vocabulary and syntax.	○	○	○
	I can explain advantages and disadvantages of ideas, plans and arrangements.	○	○	○
Writing skills	I can brainstorm, plan and draft written work with some support.	○	○	○
	I can write, edit and proofread written work with some support.	○	○	○

✓ Action plan

Reading: I need to _____

Use of English: I need to _____

Listening: I need to _____

Speaking: I need to _____

Writing: I need to _____

I would like to know more about _____

5 Friends and family

Explore
- what friends and family mean to you
- cross-cultural friendships

Create
- a letter to a relative
- a short story

Engage
- with a language student and her grandmother
- with two girls becoming friends

Collaborate
- to discuss family values
- to make a group presentation

In this chapter you will:

Reflect
- on questions
- on the use of reported speech

> There's nothing I value more than the closeness of friends and family.
> Willie Stargell, baseball player

> I believe the world is one big family, and we need to help each other.
> Jet Li, actor

> The greatest gift of life is friendship, and I have received it.
> Hubert Humphrey, politician

Friends and family

Thinking ahead

1. Spend some time thinking about your family. What do we mean by 'family'?
2. Which members of your family are you closest to? What kinds of things do you do together?
3. How do you help one another out?

Word builder

Use words from the word box to complete the sentences that follow.

| encouraging | reliable | close | support |

1. My brother and I have always been very _____.
2. Riah says what she means and is always _____.
3. Luca was grateful for the _____ his parents had always given him.
4. My best friends are great at _____ me when I find something difficult.

Speaking about friends and family

Discuss the following questions in a small group. As you discuss your opinions, try to use words and phrases you have learned from the unit so far.

1. Who comes first, family or friends? Why?
2. What makes a good friend?
3. Has there been a particular time when having a special friend/family member has been important? What happened?

Reading

📖 Letters

Read the letters below between a student and her grandmother.

Dear Gran,

I hope you're well. I think of you and miss all the family a lot, but I can't wait to tell you about the amazing time I am having here and showing you my pictures when I get back.

Alora is a wonderful little town with beautiful scenery all around. The people are so friendly, too, and are keen to help me with my Spanish. I'm so glad to have this opportunity. Last week Ana and I went to the beautiful mountain area of El Chorro.

I don't think I have told you about Ana. She's an art student from Barcelona who has been helping out on my language course. We talked a lot on the trip to El Chorro and we found we **had so much in common**. She is really close to her sister, too, just as I am to Carol – and she loves nature and the outdoors. She enjoys painting and drawing and hopes one day to be an art teacher. We are using our free days to explore the area together; we plan to visit Granada next week. Her English is excellent and I was surprised that she has never been to the UK.

That may soon change, because I have invited her to come and stay with us once our course has finished. I haven't told Mum yet, but I'm sure she won't mind. So, I hope you'll get to meet her soon! It's wonderful having a friend like Ana to **confide in**.

Lots of love,

Cathy

Dear Cathy,

Thank you for your lovely letter. I have looked up Alora on the map, so now I have some idea of where you are. Ana sounds a very nice girl and a most **suitable** friend for you, at least while you and Carol are so far apart.

Never forget your family, though. Friends are a very good thing to have, but they cannot ever replace your family.

Do get in touch as soon as you get back.

Your loving Grandmother

Glossary

had so much in common were similar / shared a lot of interests

suitable right for someone or something

confide in to share secrets with

Reading

Understanding

A Choose the correct answer to the following questions.

1. Where is Cathy staying?
   a with her grandmother
   b Alora
   c El Chorro
2. What is she there for?
   a to learn Spanish
   b to study art
   c on holiday
3. What is Cathy's sister's name?
   a Ana
   b Carol
   c we are not told

B Choose the correct answer to the following questions.

1. What do Cathy and Ana do together?
   a paint and draw
   b explore the area
   c write letters
2. Where does Cathy say they hope to go next week?
   a Granada
   b the UK
   c El Chorro

C Write answers to the following questions.

1. Write two sentences describing Cathy's friend Ana.
2. How are the two letters different in style? Give examples to back up your answer.

Challenge

Write a letter to a grandparent, or another relative, describing how you met a new friend and saying what you and that friend do together. Then read your letter to a partner.

Use of English

Questions

When we ask a question that can be answered 'yes' or 'no', we use the following word order: auxiliary/modal verb + subject + main verb.

Examples: Are you meeting your friend later?
Have you read this book?
Can you help me?

When we are asking for more information, we use question words such as 'what', 'where', 'when', 'why', 'which', 'whose', 'how', 'how many/much'. We use the word order:
question word + auxiliary/modal verb + subject + main verb.

Examples: What are you thinking?
Where do you live?
Why has he done that?
How can I help you?

To ask a negative question, we can add 'not' (usually shortened to '-n't') after the auxiliary/modal verb.

Examples: **Haven't** you done your homework?
Why **didn't** you tell me that?

Using questions

A Put the words in the correct order to make questions. Remember to add capital letters and question marks.

1. can/come/with/stay/and/you/me
2. you/do/your/time/spending/enjoy/with/family
3. didn't/meet/why/friends/you/your/school/after
4. sister/haven't/met/my/you

B Write questions for the following answers, using the words in brackets. The first one has been done for you.

1. She has one sister and one brother. (how many)
   How many brothers and sisters does she have?
2. Yes, she is my grandmother. (is)
3. She asked her friend Kiara to help her. (who)
4. Ana comes from Barcelona. (where)

C Write four questions of your own, beginning with 'Why don't', 'Hasn't', 'Whose', and 'Should'.

Remember

- In the present simple or past simple, we use a form of 'do' (do/does/did) in questions.

  Example: Do you know my sister?

- The verb 'be' comes before the subject in a question.

  Example: Is he her brother?

- The question words 'what', 'which', 'whose' and 'how much/how many' are often followed by a noun.

  Example: Which town did you visit?

Use of English

More questions

In many 'wh-' questions, the 'wh-' word is the object of the verb.

Example: What did she say?

We can also use the question words 'who', 'which', 'whose', 'what' and 'how many' as the subject of the verb in a question. The subject (the question word) comes before the verb. We do not use the auxiliary 'do/does/did'.

Examples: Who wrote this letter?
How many people went on the trip?

When we ask a 'wh-' question that contains a verb + preposition, we usually put the preposition at the end of the question.

Example: Who were you speaking **to**?

In formal writing, we sometimes put the preposition before the question word.

Examples: **In which** direction was the car travelling?
From whose point of view was the story written?
At what time does the train arrive?
To whom did you write the letter?

> **Remember**
> - If 'who' or 'what' is the subject of the verb in a question, we use a singular verb.
> - In formal language, we sometimes use 'whom' instead of 'who' as the object. After a preposition, we always use 'whom' instead of 'who'. *Example*: With whom did she go?

Using questions

A Rewrite the following questions, correcting the mistakes in the verb forms and word order.

1. How many people did go to El Chorro?
2. What did happen yesterday?
3. What about were they talking?
4. Which college goes Ana to?

B Write questions for the following answers. Use the words in brackets in the order shown.

1. Cathy was in Spain. (what/for)
2. She went to El Chorro with her friend Ana. (who/with)
3. She was writing to her grandmother. (who/to)
4. Ana lives in the city of Barcelona. (in/which)

C Write three formal questions of your own beginning 'In which …', 'To whom …' and 'At what time …'.

Listening

The importance of family

Word builder

Use the words in the word box to fill the gaps in the sentences that follow.

| golden wedding | celebration |
| respect | backpacking |

1. They had been married for fifty years and their _____ was very special.
2. The students spent the summer _____ around Europe.
3. We are having a big family _____ at New Year.
4. The people bowed their heads as a sign of _____.

Track 5.1: The importance of family

Listen to a conversation in which three students from different cultural backgrounds discuss families. Gerd from Austria has a problem, which he discusses with two friends – Agnes, who is from Zambia and Mai Ling, who is from China. When you have finished listening, answer the following questions.

Understanding

A Choose the correct answer to each of the following questions.

1. What is the name of Gerd's sister?
   a Agnes
   b Mai Ling
   c Henni
2. Where is Gerd planning to go on holiday?
   a home
   b Peru
   c somewhere with Joe and Hans
3. Why does his sister want him to go home?
   a for a family celebration
   b to have a holiday
   c to visit his Uncle Nils

Listening

B **Listen again to the conversation and then answer the following questions.**

1. Gerd says he wants advice from his two friends. What does he want them to help him with? Write a brief explanation of the problem, based on what he says to them.
2. What is their advice? For each one say briefly what they advise and why.

C Gerd, Agnes and Mai Ling each have a different view of the importance of family life. Write a brief description of each friend, saying what their views are.

💬 Speaking: What do you think?

In small groups, discuss what you think about Gerd's reasons for his views. Do you agree with his argument? If not, why not? What advice you would give him? In your discussion think about:

- what your family means to you
- any examples of family members caring for each other
- who you are particularly close to in your family
- any special events celebrated in your family.

> **Remember**
>
> Remember to ask each other questions when you are discussing. For example, to check you understand what someone has said, you can ask questions starting with 'Do you mean that …' and 'Are you saying that …'

79

Use of English

Reported statements, commands and questions

When we report what someone has said, we use a reporting verb such as 'say', 'tell' or 'explain'. When the reporting verb is in the past, we usually change the tense of the verb used by the speaker.

Example: "I **have planned** my route," Gerd told them. → Gerd told them that he **had planned** his route.

When we are reporting commands, requests or advice we use a verb such as 'tell', 'ask' or 'advise' with the 'to' infinitive.

Example: "Go home," she told him. → She **told him to go** home.

To report a question, we use reporting verbs such as 'ask', 'wonder' and 'want to know'. We make the same tense changes as in reported statements. We put the subject before the verb and we do not use the auxiliary verbs 'do/does/did'.

Example: "Did you talk to her?" she asked. → She wanted to know if he had talked to her.

Using reported speech

A Change the following statements, commands and questions into reported speech.

1. "I am trying to decide what to do," he explains.
2. "You should go backpacking some other time," Agnes advised.
3. "Think about your family," Agnes told him.
4. "Could you postpone the trip?" she asked.

B Fill the gaps in the following paragraph with the correct forms of the verbs in brackets.

Gerd asked Mai Ling and Agnes _____ (give) him some advice. He explained that he had _____ (speak) to his sister and she _____ (have) tried to persuade him to give up his holiday so that he _____ (can) go to his grandparents' celebration.

C Write five sentences of your own using the following reporting verbs: 'explained', 'told', 'asked', 'advised' and 'wanted to know'.

Remember

- When the reporting verb is in the present, we use the same tense as the original speaker.
- We do not change the following modal verbs in reported speech: would, could, should, might, ought to.
- In reported speech, 'will' becomes 'would' and 'can' becomes 'could'.

Use of English

Indirect and embedded questions

To ask for information or to make a question more polite, we often use introductory phrases such as 'Could you tell me …' and 'Do you know …'. This makes the question 'indirect'.

In indirect questions, we use the same word order as in reported questions but we do not change the tense. Look at the following examples.

Direct question	Reported question	Indirect question
"What time is it?"	She asked what time it was.	"Do you know what time it is?"
"Have you seen my pen?"	She asked if I had seen her pen.	"Could you tell me if you have seen my pen?"

Some statements have questions included or 'embedded' within them. These statements often begin with phrases such as 'I know', 'I don't know' and 'I wonder'.

Examples: I was wondering what to do.
I don't know what my friends think.

Using indirect and embedded questions

> **Remember**
> In indirect questions and in statements with embedded questions, we put the subject before the verb and we do not use the auxiliary 'do/does/did'.

A Rewrite the following questions as indirect questions using 'Could you tell me' or 'Do you know'.

1. What will you do this summer?
2. Has she visited her family recently?
3. How is she?
4. When are you arriving?

B Rewrite the following direct questions as statements using 'I wonder' or 'I don't know'. The first one has been done for you.

1. Can I go to Peru next year?
   I wonder if I can go to Peru next year.
2. What do my parents think about my plans?
3. Do my friends know how I feel?
4. Should I go to my grandparents' party?

C Choose four phrases from the box below and write indirect or embedded questions beginning with your chosen phrases.

Do you have any idea …	I don't remember …
Can you explain …	He has no idea …
Do you know …	They are not sure …

Speaking

💬 One big family?

With a partner, discuss the following questions.

1. In the quotation on page 72, Jet Li said: "I believe the world is one big family". Do you agree with him?
2. Look at the picture below. Working with your partner, how many of the flags can you identify?
3. Have you been to any of the countries represented? If so, what was it like?
4. How different from your own country was it?
5. Have you made friends with anyone from a different country and culture from your own?
6. How easy is it to be friends with someone from a different country and culture from yours? What problems might arise?

> **Remember**
>
> In your discussion, talk about family life, interests and customs.

Speaking

Group discussion and presentation

In groups of five or six you are going to discuss how you might introduce your family to a friend from another culture.

Discuss the following questions:

1. What family traditions would it be helpful for your friend to know about? (For example, the way you greet one another differs in different cultures – your friend needs to know what is polite.)

2. Are there any customs your friend might find unusual? How can you explain these to your friend? (For example, mealtimes might be very different from what your friend is used to.)

3. If you wanted your friend to spend a day with you and your family to learn what life is like for your family, what things would you include?

In your groups, prepare a presentation for the class. Make sure that everyone in your group has a chance to speak.

Reading corner

📖 **Reading corner: *Emma***

Read the following extract from Jane Austen's novel *Emma* (rewritten by Rebecca Stevens), in which the title character Emma Woodhouse makes a new friend.

Dreams

Harriet Smith was a pretty blonde girl of seventeen with round blue eyes and a look of great sweetness. She had been a pupil at Mrs Goddard's **boarding school** in the village since she was a child and had stayed on there as she had no family of her own. Emma had **known her by sight** for some time.

It was only now that she began to find her truly interesting.

Harriet wasn't clever, but she was sweet and grateful and **touchingly impressed** with everything she saw and everybody she met, especially Miss Woodhouse. Emma found her **delightful.** *With just a little help*, she thought, *some gentle advice on how to behave and the sort of friends to choose, Harriet could rise above her* **humble** *background and become quite perfect. And she, Emma, would be the one to do it!* Harriet could never take Miss Taylor's place in Emma's life, but it would be an interesting and kindly thing to do that would almost make up for the loss of her best friend.

And so Emma and Harriet Smith became friends.

Harriet visited Hartfield often and Emma liked her more each time. Harriet loved to talk and it amused Emma to listen as she **chattered** on about Mrs Goddard, the girls at school, the teachers …

Understanding

Answer the following questions.

1. Hartfield is where Emma lives. Where does Harriet live?
2. Which best describes Harriet? Choose the correct answer.
   a clever   b easily pleased   c dark haired
3. Emma has lost her best friend. What was that friend's name?
4. 'And so Emma and Harriet Smith became friends.' Write two sentences, one writing as Harriet describing her new friend and one as Emma describing Harriet.

Glossary

boarding school a school where the pupils live in
chattered talked about things that were not important
delightful pleasant, attractive
humble poor
known her by sight recognised her but did not know her name
touchingly impressed easily pleased

Writing workshop

✏️ Writing a story

You are going to plan and write a story about meeting someone for the first time.

You meet someone your own age who you have never seen before. As you start talking to this stranger you learn that you are very similar. But there are some important differences, too. Write the story of your meeting.

Planning

Begin by deciding what this stranger is like. Perhaps you could use ideas you discussed in the activities on pages 82 and 83, or you could base the person on someone you know.

Now think about your story:

- How are you going to begin the story?
- Briefly describe how you met. (For example, at a bus stop, at school, at a new sports or hobby class etc.)
- Why did you start talking to the other person?
- What did you talk about? Include some of your conversation.
- What questions did you ask?
- How did you react to the other person? Was this a new friend – or someone to avoid?
- What happens next?

Writing, editing and proofreading

Now write your story. Remember to use effective comparisons to show how this person is similar to and different from you. When you have finished, read your story to check for any mistakes in spelling or punctuation. Can you change anything to make it better? Exchange stories with a partner. Can they suggest any ways in which it can be improved?

> **Remember**
>
> Refresh your memory of comparative structures from Unit 2 (see pages 29 and 33).

Progress assessment

Progress check

Answer the following questions.

1. Use the words from the word box to write sentences of your own.

| reliable | support | closer | friends |

(4 marks)

2. What is Ana studying? Choose the correct answer.
  a Spanish   **b** art   **c** languages   (1 mark)

3. How does Cathy's grandmother describe Ana?   (1 mark)

4. Rearrange the words to form questions.
  a they/celebration/in/the/room/which/holding/are
  b with/Henni/live/who/does   (2 marks)

5. Choose the correct words from a–f to complete the following paragraph.

Gerd asks his friends for …(a)… His …(b)… are celebrating their golden wedding this year. He wants to go backpacking in …(c)… but his …(d)… thinks he should join the family …(e)… instead. His friends suggest that his …(f)… should come first.

  a advice   advise   **b** grandparents   parents
  c Zambia   Peru   **d** brother   sister
  e celebration   holiday   **f** education   family   (6 marks)

6. Gerd said his sister's ideas were old-fashioned. What does 'old-fashioned' mean?
  a very wrong   **b** too modern   **c** not modern   (1 mark)

7. What do you think Gerd will decide to do? Explain your answer.   (2 marks)

8. Rewrite these questions as reported, indirect or embedded questions using the words in brackets.
  a "What time is he coming?" (she asked)
  b "Did he go to Peru?" (I wonder)
  c "Is she going to stay with her aunt?" (Do you know)   (3 marks)

9. Does Emma like Harriet exactly the way she is? Explain your answer.   (3 marks)

10. Do you think you should ever try to change your friends? Give a reason for your answer.   (2 marks)

(Total: 25 marks)

Progress assessment

Progress assessment

		😊	😐	😟
Reading skills	I can understand implied meaning.	○	○	○
	I can read a growing range of fiction and non-fiction texts.	○	○	○
Use of English skills	I can use a range of questions, including questions containing prepositions.	○	○	○
	I can use a range of reported speech forms.	○	○	○
Listening skills	I can understand most of the detail of a person's argument.	○	○	○
	I can recognise what someone's opinion is when they are speaking.	○	○	○
Speaking skills	I can recognise inconsistencies in someone's argument when they are speaking.	○	○	○
	I can ask questions to check what someone has said.	○	○	○
	I can use a growing range of subject-specific vocabulary and syntax.	○	○	○
Writing skills	I can write, edit and proofread written work with some support.	○	○	○

Action plan

Reading: I need to _____

Use of English: I need to _____

Listening: I need to _____

Speaking: I need to _____

Writing: I need to _____

I would like to know more about _____

6 Global learning

Explore
- global issues
- e-books

Create
- a presentation
- an article

Engage
- with different points of view and opinions
- an e-author

Collaborate
- to research exchange programmes
- on a group presentation

In this chapter you will:

Reflect
- on the present perfect and past perfect
- on –ing forms and noun phrases

We may have all come on different ships, but we're in the same boat now.
Martin Luther King, civil-rights leader

Think about the kind of world you want to live and work in. What do you need to know to build the world? Demand that your teachers teach you that.
Kropotkin, author

Alone we can do so little; together we can do so much.
Helen Keller, author and activist

88

Global learning

Thinking ahead

1. Do you think it is important for schools across the world to help one another? Explain your answer.
2. In what ways can schools help one another across the world?
3. What do you think the phrase 'global communities' means?

Word builder

Match the word on the left with the definition on the right.

global	a subject or problem
community	to do with the whole world
issue	a group of people or a group in society
exchange programme	people from different countries who write to each other
pen pals	when people (often students) from two different countries visit each other

Speaking about global issues

Discuss the following questions with a partner.

1. The quotations on page 88 are about understanding that people around the world are different, but that we can work together to make the world a better place. Do you think it is important to make the world a better place today? Give reasons for your answer.
2. How can we learn more about the world we live in and make it a better place?

Remember

If you do not know a word or are not sure about a grammar point, try to find a different word or another way to explain what you want to say.

89

Reading

How e-books can help to make a global community

Read the following article and then answer the questions.

How e-books can help to make a global community

Reading makes everything possible in life; education, work and escaping **poverty**. According to UNESCO, there are 740 million **illiterate** people in this world and 250 million children of primary school age who do not have basic reading and writing skills. The Global School Community aims to bring digital books to all the children of the world and their families.

Digital technology

Digital technology is very important in helping to create a **literate** world. It can reach across the world and is fairly inexpensive. The Global School Community makes e-books available to children all around the world, either through mobile phones, tablets or computers. Technology also means that we can improve our communication skills. Distances between schools are being reduced through the use of technology, as teachers and children from schools around the world can meet online to share **resources** and discuss ideas. Remote schooling is one example of the success of communication through the Internet.

E-books

The first books a child reads can have a enormous **impact** on that child. The greater the impact, the more likely the child is to continue reading and learning throughout their life. E-books are electronic versions of printed books. E-books can educate, inform, persuade and advise. They can provide hours of entertainment and can connect schools all over the world. Studies have shown that children show great improvement in fluency and comprehension after only five months of having access to books. The Global School Community has a huge e-book library that every school has access to.

Become part of the Global School Community

The Global School Community aims to bring digital books to all children and their families, and helps schools, colleges and universities to connect with each other. Please join our family of schools, write an e-book or share resources at globalschoolcommunity.com

Glossary

illiterate unable to read or write
impact effect
literate able to read and write
poverty being extremely poor
resources materials to work with

Reading

Understanding

A **Answer the following questions.**

1. What is an e-book?
2. Why is being able to read so important?
3. Name one way that digital technology can help people around the world with reading skills.

B **Choose the correct answer to the following questions.**

1. What does the Global School Community aim to do?
   - a to make every child understand how important reading is
   - b to help teachers teach all over the world
   - c to bring digital books to all children and their families

2. Which one of the following statements is true, according to the article?
   - a Technology can improve our communication skills.
   - b Technology is a waste of time.
   - c Technology is something to be used outside school.

C **Answer the following questions.**

1. What is the evidence that e-books help children to become more literate?
2. What is the purpose of this online article?
3. What is the writer's opinion about e-books?

Writing a formal email

Write a formal email to the head teacher of your school giving reasons why money raised from a sponsored read should be given to the Global School Community. Use the information from the online article to help you. You can begin your email 'Dear Mr, Mrs or Ms … '.

Speaking: Short presentation

Using the words you learned in the Writing activity above and the information from the article, give a two-minute presentation to your classmates about how to help children all over the world learn to read and write.

Remember

Use a dictionary and thesaurus to find new words to use in your presentation.

Use of English

The present perfect

We often use the **present perfect simple** (have/has + past participle) with time words such as 'often', 'ever', 'never', 'always' and 'before' to talk about experiences in our lives up to now.

Examples: I **have read** this book **before**. It is the best book I **have ever read**.

The **present perfect continuous** (have/has + been + present participle) is often used to talk about an action that started in the past and has continued up to now.

Example: I **have been waiting** here for two hours.

Some time words can be used with the present perfect simple and continuous:

- we use 'just' and 'recently' to talk about actions in the recent past
  Examples: I **have just finished** my book. I **have just been reading** my book.
- we can use 'for' to say 'how long', and 'since' to say when an action started.
  Examples: I **have lived** here **for** five years. I **have been working** here **since** 2014.

Using the present perfect

A Use the words to write sentences in the present perfect simple.

1. I /download/e-books/several times
2. My school/never/organise/an exchange visit
3. He/always/enjoy/reading
4. My school/just/buy/some new computers

B Change the following sentences into the present perfect continuous.

1. The students have used technology to help them learn.
2. They have worked all afternoon.
3. Reena has studied English since 2012.

C Change the following sentences into the passive present perfect simple.

1. I was invited to a school in Germany next year.
2. The books were given to schools all over the world.
3. This e-book was translated into many different languages.

Remember

We make the passive form of the present perfect simple with 'have/has' + been + past participle.

Example: This letter has just been delivered.

For more information on how to make present perfect forms, see page 155.

Use of English

The past perfect

We use the **past perfect simple** (had + past participle) to talk about a completed event that happened before another event in the past.

Example: My English lesson **had** already **started** when I arrived.

We often use the past perfect in reported speech when the reporting verb is in the past.

Examples: "I have just bought a new laptop," she said. → She told me that she **had just bought** a new laptop.

We use the **past perfect continuous** (had been + present participle) to talk about an event in the past that began before a certain time and was continuing up to that time.

Example: They **had been studying** English for five years when I met them.

Using the past perfect

A Rewrite the sentences using the past perfect for the event that happened first.

1. I went to the park as soon as I finished my homework.
2. I felt excited because I applied to go on an exchange programme.
3. Before they left primary school, the students learned to read and write.

B Turn the following sentences into reported speech using the past perfect simple.

1. "I have never visited another country before," she said.
2. "I have contacted a school in Spain about the exchange programme," explained the head teacher.
3. "I organised the students' flights last week," she reminded us.

C Complete the following sentences in your own words, using the past perfect continuous.

1. When I joined this class, _____
2. I was tired because _____
3. By the time the bus came, _____

Remember

We often use the past perfect simple to show the order of events. We use the past perfect simple for the first event and the past simple for the later event.

Example: Rafia had left when I arrived. (= Rafia left and then I arrived)

For more information on how to form the past perfect, see page 155.

Listening

Writing an e-book: an interview with Harrison

Word builder

Sometimes, we may not know the exact word for something, so we need to find other words to mean the same thing. Some words used in the recording are below, together with their meanings. Can you find other words or phrases that you could use to mean the same thing?

Example: **ambition** – hope, aim, wanting success

accessible – easy to get

alternate – other

barriers – walls

evolved – changed

generate – create

incredible – amazing

inspired – encouraged

merge – mix

13-year old British-Ghanaian author Harrison Wallace.

Track 6.1: Interview with Harrison Wallace

You are going to listen to an interview with Harrison, a 13-year-old British-Ghanaian author who has lived in the UK, Ghana and Bangladesh, but now lives in Vietnam. Harrison has written an e-book, which means that it can be read by 5 million boys and girls in other countries. Listen to the interview and hear more about Harrison's book, *The Super 4: Dark Death*.

Understanding

A Choose the correct answer to each of the following questions.

1. What inspired Harrison to become an author?
    a   He had always wanted to write a book.
    b   He read a lot of books.
    c   He was asked to by his school.
2. Where was Harrison living when he wrote *The Super 4: Dark Death*?
    a   Ghana   b   Vietnam   c   Bangladesh
3. What type of novel is *The Super 4: Dark Death*?
    a   romance   b   science fiction   c   fantasy

Listening

B **Choose the correct answer to each of the following questions.**

1. How many books are in the *Super 4 series*?
   - a one
   - b four
   - c six

2. Does Harrison have plans to carry on writing?
   - a Yes, he is going to write a new science-fiction series.
   - b Yes, he is going to write a set of three fantasy novels.
   - c No, he is not going to write any more books.

3. What is Harrison's opinion about being educated in different schools and countries?
   - a He loves being in a school with people from all over the world who speak different languages.
   - b He likes the range of subjects he can study.
   - c He likes his teachers and his friends.

C **Write the answers to the following questions.**

1. What are the advantages of e-books over printed books?
2. What words of advice does Harrison give to other children who are considering becoming authors?

Writing: E-book paragraph

What genre (type) of e-book would you like to write? Make a spider diagram to plan your ideas.

Now write the first paragraph of your book. How will you get the reader's attention from the start? You could begin:

- at the end or in the middle of the story
- with a conversation
- with an event or memory
- with a powerful description of the setting
- with a shock or surprise.

Writing: E-book cover

Your new e-book is about to go on sale! Design and write the text for the cover and then show it to your classmates. Can they suggest improvements?

Glossary

author/e-author the person who writes a book/e-book

edit check and correct writing for publication

plot story

publish print a book for sale

setting the place in which a story happens

Challenge

Interview one another about the e-books you have planned in the Writing activities. Think of ten questions you could ask each other about your e-books. You could use the interview with Harrison to help with your ideas.

Think of ways of including the vocabulary that you have learned in the unit so far, including the Glossary above. When you carry out your interviews, can you find ways to carry on talking even when you don't know a word or grammar point?

Use of English

–ing forms used as nouns

We use –ing forms as part of compound nouns (see page 12), as adjectives (see page 28) and in continuous verb forms (see pages 64–65 and 92). We also use –ing forms as nouns. Compare the following examples.

Compound noun	Adjective	In a continuous verb form	As a noun
I am going to the **swimming pool**.	He was living in a **developing** country.	I **have been doing** my homework.	I enjoy **writing**.

In the example 'I enjoy writing', 'writing' is used as a noun. It is the **object** of the verb 'enjoy'. An –ing form can also be the **subject** of a verb.

Example: **Reading is** enjoyable.

We often use an –ing form as a noun after a preposition (at, in, about, of, etc.).

Examples: Harrison talked **about writing** e-books. Harrison is good **at writing**.

Using –ing forms as nouns

A Use –ing forms of the verbs in the word box to complete the sentences.

> create   become   visit   work

1. _____ a plot and characters for a story is fun.
2. He says he doesn't mind _____ hard.
3. _____ other countries can help you understand other cultures.
4. Have you ever considered _____ a writer?

> **Remember**
>
> When an –ing form is used as a noun, it is called a 'gerund'. Gerunds are always used as nouns but, like verbs, they can sometimes have an object.
>
> *Example*: Reading books can help you learn.

B Find the four –ing forms that are used as nouns in the following diary entry.

> **Diary**
>
> I heard about an amazing boy called Harrison today. He's been writing books since he was 12. If I practise my writing, maybe I'll be an author one day. I'm very keen on reading about other cultures. Learning about different countries helps Harrison when he's creating characters. I'm looking forward to finding out more about how to publish e-books.

C Complete the following sentences in your own words, using the –ing form of a verb.

1. I don't like _____
2. I am very good at _____
3. I don't mind _____

96

Use of English

Noun phrases

A noun phrase is a group of words that contains a noun and other words that tell us more about the noun. Information about the noun can come before and/or after the noun.

Noun phrases often begin with determiners or quantifiers, such as 'the', 'a/an', 'my', 'that', 'some', 'many' and 'lots of'.

Examples: **a** school, **that** book, **lots of** information

Noun phrases can also include adjectives before the noun. Adjectives come after determiners and quantifiers in a noun phrase.

Examples: a **big** school, that **new** book, lots of **useful** information

Many noun phrases include words after the noun.

Examples: that new book **which has just been published** (determiner + adjective + noun + relative clause)

lots of useful information **about e-books** (quantifier + adjective + noun + prepositional phrase)

Using noun phrases

A Use the following words to make noun phrases.

1. ideas/best/his/some of
2. school/international/visited/that/the/I
3. about/science-fiction/a different universe/novel/a

B Answer the following questions.

1. Join the two sentences using the word in brackets. The first one has been done for you.

   a Harrison wrote a novel. It was published as an e-book. (which)

   Harrison wrote a novel which was published as an e-book.

   b He has lots of friends. They can speak many languages. (who)

   c I have just read an interesting article. It was about Vietnam. (about)

   d I enjoyed my exchange visit. I visited a school in Germany. (to)

2. Write out all of the noun phrases in the answers to questions 1a–d.

C Make noun phrases using the following nouns. Include words before the noun and after the noun. Then write three sentences using the noun phrases.

school   holiday   facts

> **Remember**
>
> - Quantifiers are often followed by determiners in a noun phrase.
>
>   *Example*: many of the schools
>
> - Relative clauses begin with a relative pronoun such as 'who', 'which', 'whose' or 'that'.
>
> - A prepositional phrase is made with a preposition + noun, pronoun or noun phrase.

Speaking

💬 Speaking about different schools

Look at the photographs of different schools and then answer the questions below.

💬 Speaking about different schools

Discuss the following questions with a partner.

1. What are some of the differences between these schools?
2. Which of the schools pictured would you like to go to and why?
3. How would you describe your own school?

Speaking

💬 Exchange programmes: Group research

In groups, you are going to carry out research about different exchange programmes. (You will then present the information you have researched in the activity below.)

First, research information on different exchange programmes. These could be exchanges within schools and universities or study or work experiences. You could use the Internet and/or speak to your teachers to find out if the school has been involved in any exchange activities. Decide as a group, how you will divide up the research.

When the group has carried out the research, decide together which exchange programme you would like to focus on for your presentation (see below). If you wish, you can design your own exchange programme between schools based on your research.

> **Remember**
>
> When you discuss your opinions with your group, try to use some of the vocabulary you have learned from the unit so far.

💬 Exchange programmes: Group presentation

When your group has completed the research, plan a presentation for the class. What information will you include in your presentation? Discuss your opinions with your group and decide how to divide up the presentation. Each person in the group should have a chance to speak for between one and two minutes.

You will need to think about the following:

- How will you introduce the exchange programme?
- Does it have a specific purpose?
- How does it work? What new things will people learn?
- Discuss the advantages and the disadvantages of the exchange programme.
- Allow time at the end for questions and answers.

Reading corner

📖 Reading corner: Article to persuade

There are many world issues that affect us all. You are going to read an article on the global theme of water. Read the article carefully and then answer the questions that follow.

Glossary

crisis a time of great difficulty

partnership when two people or organisations work together

raise awareness tell people

reality the way things are

Water – a global issue

The water crisis

Can you *imagine life* without safe water to drink? For millions of people, this is a *daily reality*. 500 million people don't have access to safe water. They have no choice but to drink dirty water that could kill them.

Everyone has the right to clean water and a right to a bright future. Women and girls often have to walk for miles to collect dirty water that prevents them from gaining an education, later getting a job and achieving their dreams.

What can be done?

We must:
- improve access to safe water
- make governments aware of the **crisis**
- make governments recognise that access to safe water is important.

What can schools do?

Schools can join together to **raise awareness** of the global issue of water. The campaigns 'Water is Precious, don't waste it' and 'Think, Stop, Tap' have been launched in 5,000 schools all over the world.

Success stories

Treetops School in Norway has been a partner with The Way School in Zimbabwe for five years now. Both schools have learned many things from one another and both have raised money to fund clean water in The Way School. Head teacher Mr Abase Okonjo said, "The **partnership** has brought knowledge, education and understanding to both schools. We have clean water and I feel the life chances of all my students have been improved."

So that's what other people are doing to address the water crisis. What can *you* do?

Understanding

Answer the following questions.

1. Who does the article say we need to make aware of the crisis?
2. Why is water a global issue?
3. In what ways are girls and women particularly affected?
4. List three features used in the layout of this online article.
5. Give three examples of language to persuade.

Writing workshop

Writing an article to persuade

You are going to plan and write a persuasive online article on a global theme of your choice. It should be something that schools could work together on. Use the guidance provided to help you.

Planning

Research online global issues that could be of interest to schools around the world.

1. Which global issue can you research? For example: the environment, education for all, climate change, pollution, energy or endangered species.
2. Why is it an issue? Can you include facts and statistics?
3. What can schools do to help?
4. What can be done in the future?
5. How can you write your article and develop your argument in a way that will persuade the reader?
6. What layout will you use for your article?

Before you write your article, think about:

- audience – who are you writing for?
- facts – include important information and facts from your research
- opinion – what is your opinion? It should be clear and strong throughout the article.
- persusasive language – how can you persuade your reader and keep them interested? Can you use emotive language to appeal to their sympathy, statistics to strengthen your argument, rhetorical questions, repetition?

Writing, editing and proofreading

Now write your online article on a global issue. Write about 150–250 words.

When you have finished, read through your article. Have you included techniques to persuade the reader and information? Check your spelling and correct any mistakes you have made. Then share your article with a partner. Can they suggest any ways to improve it?

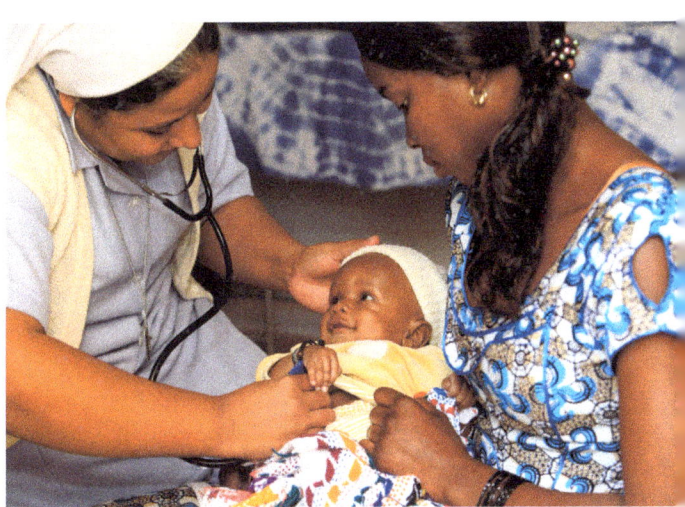

Progress assessment

Progress check

Answer the following questions.

1. Choose the correct answer. According to the article on page 90, e-books can …
   - a help children relax.
   - b help children connect with one another.
   - c educate, inform, persuade and advise. (1 mark)

2. List three forms of technology children can use to access e-books. (3 marks)

3. Fill the gaps in the following sentences with 'for' or 'since'.
   - a We have been waiting here _____ three hours.
   - b A lot has happened _____ I last saw you. (2 marks)

4. Choose the correct words from a–e to complete the following paragraph about Track 6.1.

   Harrison is the …(a)… of a new …(b)… His …(c)… novel is about …(d)… living in an …(e)… world.

a	illustrator	author	reader
b	e-book	printed book	interview
c	scientific	science-fiction	non-fiction
d	children	teenagers	e-authors
e	ordinary	real-life	amazing

   (5 marks)

5. Did Harrison always want to be an author? Explain your answer. (2 marks)

6. Do you think Harrison believes that reading is important? Give a reason for your answer. (2 marks)

7. Use the correct form of the verb in brackets to fill the gap in the following sentence.

   Harrison is very interested in _____ about other cultures. (learn) (1 mark)

8. Find the noun phrases in the following sentences.
   - a Binta found some useful facts about global issues.
   - b She wrote an excellent article which included lots of information. (2 marks)

9. Name four benefits of schools across the world working together. (4 marks)

10. List three features of an article to persuade. (3 marks)

(Total: 25 marks)

Progress assessment

Progress assessment

		😊	😐	😟
Reading skills	I can understand the detail of an argument.	○	○	○
	I can recognise a writer's attitude or opinion.	○	○	○
Use of English skills	I can use the present perfect, including some passive forms.	○	○	○
	I can use the past perfect.	○	○	○
	I can use a range of gerunds and noun phrases.	○	○	○
Listening skills	I can understand most of the specific points that someone is saying.	○	○	○
	I can recognise what someone's opinion is when they are speaking.	○	○	○
Speaking skills	I can explain my own point of view.	○	○	○
	I can think of other ways to say something if I have gaps in my knowledge.	○	○	○
	I can work with others to agree and organise ways to complete tasks.	○	○	○
	I can use a growing range of subject-specific vocabulary.	○	○	○
Writing skills	I can develop arguments in my writing.	○	○	○
	I can use the correct style, register and layout.	○	○	○

✓ Action plan

Reading: I need to _____

Use of English: I need to _____

Listening: I need to _____

Speaking: I need to _____

Writing: I need to _____

I would like to know more about _____

7 History around us

Explore
- the story of everyday objects
- famous inventions

Create
- a paragraph about the history of an everyday object
- an acrostic poem

Engage
- with students discussing inventions
- with poems

Collaborate
- to talk about famous inventions
- to discuss a time capsule for your school

In this chapter you will:

Reflect
- on conjunctions
- on infinitives and –ing forms

If you would understand anything, observe its beginning and its development.
Aristotle, ancient Greek philosopher

Anyone can look for history in a museum. The creative historian looks for history in a hardware store.
Robert S Wieder, author

Necessity is the mother of invention.
Proverb

History around us

Thinking ahead

1. Take some time to look around you. Write a list of the everyday objects you can see.
2. Do you know the history of any of the objects you have listed? How have they developed to be what they are now?
3. Think of some important inventions that have become part of our daily lives.

Word builder

Use words from the word box to complete the sentences below.

| metal | material | plastic | wooden | cardboard |

1. Our new television was packed in a big _____ box.
2. Bank cards are made of _____.
3. Check the objects to see what _____ each one is made from.
4. The knife had a _____ handle made from an olive tree and its _____ cutting edge was very sharp.

Speaking about everyday objects

Discuss the following questions with a partner. See how many words you can use from the Word builder.

1. Look again at the list of everyday objects you made in the Thinking ahead activity. What is each object made of?
2. The proverb at the bottom of page 104 is an expression that means if you really need something, you will find a way to get it. Do you agree? Explain your answer.

105

Reading

📖 Paper, pens and pencils

Read the article below, which explains the history of paper, pens and pencils.

Paper, pens and pencils

As you read this page, you probably have in front of you some paper, a pen and at least one pencil. Have you ever wondered how they were first made and where they come from?

Paper

The word 'paper' comes from the name '**papyrus**', a reed-like plant. The ancient Egyptians took the soft centre of this plant and added water to make a wet mixture or pulp, which was then pressed together and hung up to dry. The resulting sheet was strong yet **flexible** and was used as writing material in Greek and Roman times. However, it was the Chinese who invented what we now know as paper. The method, in use over 2,000 years ago, also involved pressing and drying wet material to form sheets. A variety of ingredients were used and these included the **bark** of certain trees. It was not until the 19th century that paper became cheap to make and easily available.

Pens

The earliest pens were **hollow** reeds that were dipped into dye, or ink, to produce a rough form of writing. By the 6th century BCE, feathers had replaced the reeds and feathers continued to be used until the development of the metal **nib**. The ballpoint pen was developed in the second half of the 20th century by the Hungarian Biro brothers. Their name gave us the term 'biro' that we use today.

Pencils

From the time of the Romans, a metal **rod**, made of lead (a soft metal), was used to write on papyrus. The lead left only a light mark and was later replaced by another soft metal, called **graphite**. Unlike lead, graphite was not poisonous and produced a much firmer, heavier line. The graphite rods, however, broke very easily and so they were wrapped in string, which made a rather weak pencil. Then an Italian couple, the Bernacottis, invented something a little like our modern pencil by hollowing out **twigs** to contain the graphite. These in turn were replaced by hollow tubes of wood, more like the pencils we use today.

Glossary

bark the hard outer part of a tree

flexible able to change shape without breaking

graphite a soft metal used in pencils

hollow having a hole or empty space inside

nib the pointed end of a pen

papyrus a reed-like plant and a form of writing material made from it

rod a thin, straight stick

twigs the small branches of a tree

Reading

Understanding

A Answer the following questions.

1. Use words from the Glossary on page 106 to complete these sentences.

   a The _____ in the pencil made a clear mark on the paper.

   b An early writing material made by the ancient Egyptians was called _____.

   c She dipped the _____ in the ink and began to write.

   d A sheet of plastic is strong but _____.

   e The tree trunk was covered in white _____.

   f He picked up some _____ that had fallen from the tree.

2. Who invented the biro? Choose the correct answer.

   a two Romans   **b** two Hungarians   **c** two Italians

3. What is in the centre of a modern pencil? Choose the correct answer.

   a lead   **b** graphite   **c** string

B Choose the correct answer to the following questions.

1. In which century did paper become readily available?

   a the 6th   **b** the 19th   **c** the 20th

2. Why did pencil makers change from lead to graphite?

   a Graphite was poisonous.
   b Graphite broke more easily.
   c Graphite made darker lines.

3. What change did the Bernacottis introduce?

   a They used twigs instead of string.
   b They used twigs instead of graphite.
   c They used string instead of graphite.

C Write three sentences, one each on the history of paper, pens and pencils.

> **Challenge**
>
> Choose one of the everyday items below and, in pairs, research its history in a library or on the Internet. Then use your research to write a paragraph about it. In small groups, read your paragraphs to each other. Choose from:
> - paper clip
> - rubber band
> - drawing pin
> - scissors
> - sticky tape.

Use of English

Conjunctions

We use the conjunctions 'because', 'since' and 'as' to talk about the **reasons and causes** of a situation or action. We can use 'so' to talk about the **results**.

Examples:

I can't print this document **because** I don't have any paper.

I don't have any paper **so** I can't print this document.

To talk about the **purpose** of an action, we often use the conjunctions 'so (that)' and 'in order that'. The clause that follows often includes 'can', 'could', 'will' or 'would'.

Example: I am going to buy some paper **so (that)** I can print this document.

We also use 'to' and 'in order to' to talk about the purpose of an action.

Example: I went out **(in order) to buy** some paper.

Remember

- Conjunctions are linking words that we use to join clauses in a sentence.
- 'Because', 'since' and 'as' can come at the beginning or in the middle of a sentence.
- We usually use 'so', 'so that' and 'in order that' in the middle of a sentence.

Using conjunctions

A Complete the following sentences with a conjunction from the box.

> so   because   so that

1. My pencil isn't sharp _____ I've been using it all morning.
2. I want to draw a picture _____ I need to find a pencil.
3. I went to the shop _____ I could buy a new pen.

B Join the two sentences using the words in brackets. The first one has been done for you.

1. I printed the article. I wanted to show it to my friend. (so that/could)

   I printed the article so that I could show it to my friend.

2. I'm going to the museum. I want to see some papyrus. (so that/can)
3. I did some research. I wanted to find out more about paper. (in order to)
4. Lead wasn't safe. It was replaced by graphite. (so)

C Write three sentences of your own using 'so that', 'in order that' and 'in order to'.

Use of English

More conjunctions

We use the conjunctions 'but' and 'although' to show a **contrast** or a **difference** between the facts and ideas in a sentence. We often use 'although' when the difference is unexpected or surprising.

Examples:

I enjoy fiction, **but** I prefer books about science.

Although the exam was quite hard, I got full marks!

He reads lots of books **although** he says he doesn't like reading.

In more formal writing, we sometimes use 'while' or 'whereas'.

Example: In the past, feather quills were often used for writing, **while/whereas** today we often use pens with metal nibs.

Using conjunctions

A Complete the following sentences with one of the clauses below. Join the two clauses with 'although' or 'but'.

| I want to print some photos | it remained expensive until the 19th century |
| I have a computer | I usually send emails |

1. Paper was invented over 2,000 years ago _____
2. I sometimes write letters by hand, _____
3. _____, I have run out of paper.
4. _____, I prefer to write letters with a pen and paper.

Remember
- 'But' usually goes in the middle of a sentence.
- We can use 'although' at the beginning or in the middle of a sentence.

B Join the following sentences using the most suitable conjunction from the brackets.

1. We use paper to write on. It also has many other uses. (so/but/since)
2. The ancient Egyptians invented papyrus. Paper was invented in China. (since/as/whereas)
3. Papyrus was made from a reed-like plant. Modern paper is usually made from wood pulp. (because/so/while)

C Write three sentences of your own using the conjunctions 'although', 'while' and 'whereas'.

109

Listening

Great inventions

Word builder

Use the words or phrases from the word box to fill the gaps in the sentences below.

| pitch black | electricity | invention |
| candles | sunset | |

1. In the past, people made light by burning blocks of wax called _____.
2. We use _____ to heat and light our homes.
3. The night was _____ and we could see nothing.
4. "I think the Internet is the greatest _____ of all time," said Jose.
5. My favourite time of day is around _____.

Track 7.1: Inventions

You are going to listen to a conversation in which a group of students suddenly find themselves in complete darkness. While they are waiting for the lights to come back on, they talk about the invention of light bulbs. Read the words and their meanings in the Glossary and then listen to the recording and answer the questions.

Glossary

filament the part of a light bulb that is heated to make light

incandescent giving off light as a result of being heated

power cut temporary failure in the supply of electricity

Listening

Understanding

A Choose the correct answer to each of the following questions.

1. Why do the lights go out?
   a There is a power cut.
   b Marco can't find the switch.
   c It is pitch black.
2. Why does Marco produce candles?
   a because they smell nice
   b because they will give some light
   c because they don't give much light
3. What was Sacha's science project about?
   a the invention of the light bulb
   b the invention of the telephone
   c the invention of electricity
4. How would you describe the language used in the recording?
   a Informal, because the students make jokes.
   b Formal, because they discuss the history of the light bulb.
   c Informal, because they use contractions and don't always speak in full sentences.

B Listen to the recording again and then answer the following questions.

1. What happened in 1835?
2. What improvements did Edison introduce to the light bulb?

C Why does Joni choose the light bulb as the best invention?

💬 Speaking: Great inventions

In small groups, discuss whether you agree with Joni. If not, what would you have chosen and why? Think about:
- the difference having good light at night makes
- other inventions that have changed people's lives
- everyday things that you would find it hard to do without.

Use of English

Infinitives after adjectives and verbs

We use the 'to' infinitive after many adjectives, especially adjectives that give an opinion or tell us how someone thinks or feels.

Examples: It's **hard to play** the violin.   I am **pleased to see** you.

Other adjectives that are followed by a 'to' infinitive include: easy, likely, impossible, possible, amazed, anxious, delighted, difficult, disappointed, glad, happy, keen, lucky, shocked, sorry, surprised, willing.

We also use the 'to' infinitive after many verbs.

Example: They **arranged to meet** in the evening.

Other verbs that are followed by the 'to' infinitive include: aim, appear, attempt, deserve, intend, manage, need, prepare, pretend, seem, try, want, wish.

Sometimes an object comes before the 'to' infinitive.

Example: Marco **advised them to wait** for the power to come back on.

Other verbs that are followed by an object and the 'to' infinitive include: allow, cause, encourage, force, invite, persuade, remind, tell, teach, warn.

Using the 'to' infinitive

A Use a word from the box and the correct form of the verb in brackets to complete the sentences.

| delighted | tried | impossible | persuaded |

1. They _____ the lights. (turn on)
2. Joni _____ them _____ inventions. (talk about)
3. Luka said it's _____ electricity. (invent)
4. They were _____ the lights come on again. (see)

Remember

To make a negative, we put 'not' in front of 'to'.
Example: We decided not to go.

B Write the words in the correct order to make sentences.

1. difficult/the/see/in/dark/to/it's
2. to/candles/managed/Marco/some/find
3. light bulbs/talk/Joni/keen/was/to/about
4. reminded/the lights/to/them/not/leave/on/he

C Complete the following sentences in your own words using the 'to' infinitive.

1. I was disappointed _____
2. He deserved _____
3. She encouraged _____

Use of English

Verbs + –ing forms

After some verbs, we use the **–ing form** of the verb rather than the 'to' infinitive.

Example: They **enjoyed talking** about inventions.

Other verbs that are followed by –ing forms include: admit, avoid, consider, dislike, finish, imagine, involve, mention, mind, miss, practise, suggest.

Some verbs can be followed by the 'to' infinitive or an –ing form. These verbs include: begin, continue, hate, like, love, prefer, start.

Examples: They **continued talking**. They **continued to talk**.

We also use the –ing form after verbs that are followed by prepositions.

Example: I am **looking forward to seeing** you.

Other verbs + prepositions that are followed by the –ing form include: admit to, agree with, apologise for, believe in, complain about, decide against, dream about/of, give up, insist on, keep on, put off, succeed in, think about, worry about.

Using verbs + –ing forms

A Use the correct forms of both the verbs in brackets to complete the following sentences.

1. When the lights went out, they _____ the party. (consider/postpone)
2. He arrived after everyone else, so he _____ late. (apologise for/be)
3. Scientists _____ things all the time. (keep on/improve)

B Complete the sentences below using the correct form of the verb in brackets ('to' infinitive or –ing).

1. Do you remember _____ about electricity? (learn)
2. Don't forget _____ some light bulbs when you go shopping. (buy)
3. They'll never forget _____ the evening in the dark. (spend)

C Complete the following sentences using an –ing form of a verb of your choice.

1. They succeeded in _____
2. Can you imagine _____
3. He complained about _____

> **Remember**
>
> The verbs 'forget', 'remember', 'regret' and 'stop' can be followed by a 'to' infinitive or an –ing form, but the meaning is different.
>
> *Examples*: I remembered to bring my ticket.
> I remember meeting your brother.

113

Speaking

Time capsule

Sometimes, when a new building is built, everyday objects are buried in the ground underneath it on purpose. This is done so that people in the future can find out what life was like in the past. The objects are put in a box or a special tube called a capsule.

The items are carefully chosen and might include the following:

💬 Time capsule

In pairs, look at the pictures above and discuss the following questions.

1. Why do you think people like to bury time capsules? Think about:
   - what the items in the capsule represent
   - why you might want people in the future to know what life is like now.

2. Why do you think each object pictured has been chosen? Think about:
   - How does a newspaper give an idea of everyday life?
   - What does the money show?
   - Why is a toy chosen?
   - What will a diary show?

Speaking

Word builder

Use the words or phrases from the word box to fill the gaps in the paragraph below.

| tube | important | selected | time capsule |

The class worked together to make a _____. They wanted things that were _____ to them to be included. Each member of the group _____ at least one object. These items were placed in a metal _____, which was then carefully closed and buried under the new building.

A time capsule for your school

Your school is going to have a new building. Someone has suggested burying a time capsule underneath it.

In groups, discuss the following questions:

- Why might this be a good idea? Brainstorm as many reasons as you can.
- What general impression of your school life would you want to give?
- What objects do you think should be included? Think of as many different things as you can.

Now discuss the list of objects together. Each member of the group should choose one item and give a short talk to the group explaining their choice.

Reading corner: 'Light bulb'

You are going to read a short poem that describes what happens when a light bulb is lit up. The light bulb is not actually mentioned in the poem – or is it? Read the poem and then answer the questions that follow.

Light bulb

Lengthening shadows
In the gathering gloom
Getting ever darker
Here's a silent room …
Tiptoe to the light switch
Bring an end to night
Undo all the darkness
Let a magic moment
Bathe the room in light

Glossary

bathe cover an area in something

darkness the state of being dark

gathering gloom an area that is getting darker

lengthening growing longer

tiptoe walk very quietly on your toes

undo end, put a stop to

Understanding

Answer the following questions.

1. What time of day is the poem describing?
2. Why do you think the room is silent?
3. What is the magic moment?
4. Why do you think it is described as 'magic'?
5. How is the light bulb mentioned in the poem?

Writing workshop

✏️ Writing an acrostic poem

'Light bulb' is an example of an acrostic poem. An acrostic poem is one where the first letter of each line spells out a word or short sentence.

Example:

>**P**en and paper
>**O**n the table
>**E**ncourage me to
>**M**ake a poem!

You are going to write an acrostic poem. Each line needs to begin with a letter of a word so that the whole poem spells out that word vertically (reading downwards).

Practice

Begin by making up some short acrostics. Choose a day of the week and write it vertically down the page. Then write a word starting with each letter in turn.

Example:

>**M**onday
>**O**rganise
>**N**ew
>**D**ay
>**A**wake?
>**Y**es

Now try and write more than one word on each line.

Writing and proofreading

Choose one of the following as the subject of your acrostic poem:

WHEEL   CLOCK   PENCIL   SCISSORS

Don't just write down any words that happen to begin with the right letter. Try to say something about the object and what it does. When you have completed your poem, proofread what you have written for accuracy. Then read your poem to your partner. Can they suggest any improvements?

117

Progress check

Answer the following questions.

1. Fill in the gaps using each of the words in the box.

   > material   plastic   wooden

   The handles were made of clear _____, which was a stronger _____ than the old _____ ones. (3 marks)

2. What were the earliest pens made from? Choose the correct answer.
   - a feathers
   - b reeds
   - c papyrus (1 mark)

3. Which of these objects is flexible? Choose the correct answer.
   - a a rock
   - b a glass
   - c a plastic ruler (1 mark)

4. Choose the correct conjunction from the brackets to complete these sentences.
   - a _____ plastic is strong, it's also flexible. (Because/While/So)
   - b I took my money with me _____ I could buy some paper. (although/so that)
   - c The engine was broken, _____ the car wouldn't start. (to/so/because) (3 marks)

5. Write a short paragraph to describe what happens in Track 7.1. (4 marks)

6. Why were light bulbs little used before Edison's invention? Give two reasons. (2 marks)

7. Fill in the gaps with the correct form of the verbs in brackets.
   - a They gave up _____ to turn on the lights. (to try/trying)
   - b He's putting off _____ his next party. (to arrange/arranging)
   - c We need _____ the light bulb. (changing/to change) (3 marks)

8. What is placed in a time capsule? Choose the correct answer.
   - a clocks
   - b everyday items
   - c medicine (1 mark)

9. Explain what an acrostic poem is. (1 mark)

10. Write an acrostic poem about an everyday object of your choice. (6 marks)

(Total: 25 marks)

Progress assessment

		😊	😐	😟
Reading skills	I can understand specific points in a text.	○	○	○
	I can recognise typical features in written texts.	○	○	○
Use of English skills	I can use conjunctions.	○	○	○
	I can use infinitives and –ing forms.	○	○	○
Listening skills	I can understand most of the detail of a person's argument.	○	○	○
	I can recognise what someone's opinion is when they are speaking.	○	○	○
Speaking skills	I can recognise typical features when someone is speaking.	○	○	○
	I can explain my own point of view.	○	○	○
	I can use a growing range of subject-specific vocabulary and syntax.	○	○	○
Writing skills	I can use the appropriate layout for a range of written genres.	○	○	○
	I can compose, edit and proofread written work at text level.	○	○	○

✓ Action plan

Reading: I need to _____

Use of English: I need to _____

Listening: I need to _____

Speaking: I need to _____

Writing: I need to _____

I would like to know more about _____

8 Food in the future

Explore
- possible future foods
- why we might need to think about food in the future

Create
- a story
- food blogs set in the future

Engage
- with two chefs of the future
- with a blogger and a scientist

Collaborate
- to make an advertisement for a class competition
- to make clear and reasoned arguments

In this chapter you will:

Reflect
- on future forms
- on modal forms

The best time to plant a tree is 20 years ago. The second best time is now.
Anonymous

Pull up a chair. Take a taste. Come join us. Life is so endlessly delicious.
Ruth Reichl, food writer

If we do not permit the earth to produce beauty and joy, it will in the end not produce food, either.
Joseph Wood Krutch, environmentalist

Food in the future

💭 Thinking ahead

1. How do you think food might change in the future?
2. What can we learn about food from the past?
3. What role could the environment and farming play in food for the future?

🧩 Word builder

Look at the advertisement below introducing a new fruit. Rewrite the advertisement, using words from the word box to fill in the gaps.

| peach | taste | brand-new |
| strawberry | delicious | grape |

STRAWGRAPE

Introducing the _____ fruit – the S T R A W G R A P E!
Part _____ part _____ **and** part _____,
its _____ _____ will make your
mouth water. Buy NOW!

💬 Speaking about food in the future

Discuss the following questions with a partner.

1. Which fruits would you use to make a new 'super fruit' like the 'strawgrape'?
2. What adjectives could you use to describe your new fruit?
3. Do you think it is important to develop new types of food? Explain your answer.

121

Reading

📖 Finding foods for the future

Read the following article and then answer the questions.

Finding foods for the future

Meet dulse, a **seaweed** with a secret.

This **translucent** red **alga** grows along [the northern coasts] of the Atlantic and Pacific oceans. And its colourful, leathery **fronds** hide a **remarkable** flavour …

"I think it is a food of the future," says Chris Langdon. This **marine** scientist has been studying dulse for more than a decade at Oregon State University in Portland. During that time, he has found new ways to grow it faster. The alga not only grows cheaply and easily, he notes, but also is rich in protein …

People need to **seek out** new foods because the world has so many mouths to feed. As of 2015, there are more than seven billion people on Earth, according to the United Nations. And by 2100 that number may double, according to some predictions. Feeding all of these people means not only improving the way food is grown, but also finding new **sources** of **nutrition**.

And that **quest** is becoming ever more urgent. If nothing changes, within 35 years, the world's **appetite** will be greater than the amount of food produced.

Glossary

alga a simple plant

appetite the feeling that makes you want to eat something

fronds leaves

marine to do with the sea

nutrition the food that people eat and the way it makes a difference to their health

quest an attempt to find something or do something difficult

remarkable very unusual or surprising

seaweed a plant found in the sea

seek out look for

sources places things come from

translucent see-through

Reading

Understanding

A Choose the correct answer to the following questions.

1. What kind of food is dulse?
   - a fruit
   - b vegetable
   - c seaweed

2. For how long has Chris Langdon been studying dulse?
   - a more than ten years
   - b less than ten years
   - c exactly ten years

B Answer the following questions.

1. Write two ways to describe what dulse looks like.
2. Why do new foods need to be developed, according to the article?

C Answer the following questions.

1. Explain what 'the world's appetite will be greater than the amount of food produced' means in your own words.
2. How does the writer of the article back up their argument? Give an example.
3. Do you think the writer's argument is a strong one? Could they be wrong about the future of food? If so, how?

Speaking: Food in the year 3020

Imagine it is the year 3020 – food will probably have changed a lot! Talk about the following ideas with a partner:

- What new foods have been discovered?
- Do we still eat in the same way?
- What are restaurants in 3020 like?

Challenge

Imagine that you are a food critic in 3020 and you are going to write a review of a meal that you have just eaten. What layout will you use for your review? You may want to use subheadings such as Restaurant, Starter, Main course, Dessert, My opinion, Price, The verdict, or you may choose to write a blog – it is up to you. Remember, this is set in the future, so you can be creative with the layout and what you choose to write.

Remember

Focus on ways to carry on your conversation even when you find gaps in your knowledge of vocabulary or grammar. Think of other words you can use that have a similar meaning and think of different ways to use grammar.

Use of English

Talking about the future

To talk about the future, we often use **will** or **shall + verb**. We often use this form:

- to talk about future facts and predict things we believe to be true about the future; if we are not certain, we often use 'will' with 'I think', 'maybe' or 'probably'

    Example: Some people think the world's population **will double** by 2100.

- to talk about offers, promises and decisions we make at the time of speaking.

    Examples: **Shall I pick** you **up**? **I'll take** you home. **I'll have** the soup, please.

When we are speaking, we often use **be going to + verb** instead of 'will' to predict things and to talk about decisions and plans we have already made.

Example: Today, we are **going to talk about** new kinds of food.

To make passive forms, we use 'will be' + past participle or 'am/is/are going to' + past participle.

Examples: Different kinds of food **will be needed** in the future.

The menu **is going to be printed** tomorrow.

Using future forms

A Fill the gaps in the following conversation with the most appropriate future form, 'will/won't' or 'going to'.

Abi: I've decided. I'm _____ try some dulse tomorrow.

Saskia: Do you think you _____ like the flavour?

Abi: I hope so! Are you _____ come to the restaurant with us?

Saskia: No, I'm _____ have dinner with my aunt.

Abi: So I probably _____ see you until Thursday.

Saskia: No, but I _____ call you tomorrow.

B Change the following sentences into the passive. The first one has been done for you.

1. Will many people eat dulse in the future?

    Will dulse be eaten by many people in the future?

2. Scientists will probably develop new kinds of food.
3. They are going to add dulse to the menu.
4. Maybe they will serve the dulse with rice.
5. More farmers will probably grow dulse in the future.

Remember

- Instead of 'will not' we often say 'won't'.
- With 'I' and 'we', we often use 'shall' instead of 'will', especially in formal speaking and writing.
- When we are speaking, we often shorten 'will' and 'shall' to –'ll.

    Example: I'll see you tomorrow.

Farming dulse

Use of English

More ways to talk about the future

To talk about the future, we can also use:

- the **present continuous** for future plans and arrangements we have made

    Examples: Who**'s making** dinner tonight? I**'m seeing** my aunt tomorrow.

- the **present simple** for planned events and arrangements that are fixed or part of a timetable.

    Examples: What time **does** the restaurant **open**? The restaurant **opens** at 6 o'clock.

We use the **future continuous** to talk about things that will be happening at a particular time or over a period of time in the future. To form the future continuous, we use will + be + present participle (the –ing form).

Example: This time tomorrow, we**'ll be having** dinner at the restaurant.

Using future forms

A Ali and Reena are chefs who work for the same chain of restaurants. Fill the gaps in their conversation using present continuous or present simple forms of the verbs in brackets.

Ali: We _____ (have) a meeting to discuss the new menu. Most of the chefs _____ (come). Is Thursday convenient for you?

Reena: I'm not sure. I _____ (hold) some interviews for a new chef on Thursday morning.

Ali: The meeting _____ (start) at 2 o'clock.

Reena: Okay, that's fine for me. The last interview _____ (be) at 12.

B Use future continuous forms of verbs in the box to complete the following sentences.

    eat   discuss   prepare   think

1. I can't go out on Wednesday evening. I _____ for my interview.
2. The chefs _____ the new menu on Thursday afternoon.
3. I _____ of you on Thursday morning. Good luck!
4. In 50 years' time, people _____ new kinds of food.

Challenge

Complete the following sentences with your own words using the future continuous.

1. This time on Saturday, I _____
2. In ten years' time, I _____
3. By the time I'm 30, I _____

125

Listening

Conversation between two chefs in the year 3020

🎧 **Track 8.1 Two chefs discuss their menu in the year 3020**

You are going to listen to a conversation between two chefs, Zach and Boni, deciding on a menu in the year 3020. Before you listen, discuss with a partner what you think they might talk about. Then read the words and their meanings in the Glossary and listen to the recording.

Glossary
floating moving through the air
grain a crop such as wheat
gratin a dish made with breadcrumbs and cheese
locusts grasshoppers
production when you make or grow something

Understanding

A Choose the correct answer to each of the following questions.

1. Why are the two chefs meeting?
   a to decide on the menu for tonight
   b to cook the food for tonight
   c to prepare the food for tonight

2. How do customers choose their food at the restaurant?
   a They order from a waiter or waitress.
   b They click on a floating picture of the dish.
   c They write their orders down.

3. Which dessert has been very popular?
   a Cream of Carrot
   b Blue Melon
   c Leaves and Ants

4. Which of the following sentences about the recording is **not** correct?
   a The language used is informal.
   b There are clues that the recording is set in the future.
   c The chefs speak formally because they are work colleagues.

Listening

B Answer the following questions.

1. Zach says he is going to 'fly the aerobike' to pick up the food. What do you think this means?

2. Here are some of the main dishes the chefs were discussing. For each letter in brackets, choose the correct word from a-c below.

> Seaweed and ...(a)... Bake – A delicious mix of seaweed and ...(a)... baked in the oven.
>
> Lemon ...(b)... – ...(b)... fried with lemon to create a light summer dish.
>
> ...(c)... Gratin – ...(c)... served in a mouth-watering breadcrumb and cheese bake.

a	plant	grass	graze
b	insects	locusts	beetles
c	seed	grain	grape

3. Which of the following statements would Zach say about the past?
   a "It's sad that people chose their own food."
   b "It's unbelievable to think people could choose what they ate."
   c "Why would people choose their own food?"

C Answer the following questions.

1. What caused the Great Hunger of 2040?
2. Do Zach and Boni have a choice about what food they serve in the restaurant? Explain your answer.

✏️ Writing: *The Great Hunger of 2040*

Write the beginning of a story called *The Great Hunger of 2040*.

You can begin it like this: '5th December 2040. I will never forget this day ...'.

⭐ Challenge

Complete the story you have begun about the Great Hunger of 2040. How can you engage the reader's interest? Think about the layout you will use for your story.

127

Use of English

Modal verbs

We can use modal verbs before other verbs to say that someone **is able** to do something, to say that something is **certain, likely** or **possible**, to say that something is **necessary** or **has to be done**, and to make **requests**.

ability	can/can't
	Example: She **can** speak English.
certain	will/won't, shall/shan't, must, can't/couldn't
	Examples: I **will** see you later. You **must** be very tired. He **can't** be in Italy – I saw him ten minutes ago.
likely or possible	*likely*: should, ought to *possible*: may (not), might (not), could
	Examples: They **should** be there. I **might** see you later. I suppose he **could** be her brother.
necessary / has to be done	must
	Example: I **must** arrive on time for my exam.
requests	will, would, can, could
	Examples: **Can** you help me? **Would** you mind opening the door?

Using modal forms

A Choose the correct modal verb from the brackets to complete each of the following sentences.

1. There are lots of people in town. It _____ be a busy night in the restaurant. (won't/can't/should)
2. Please _____ you add the ingredients to the menu? (should/could/must)
3. All customers _____ pay for their food before they leave. (must/won't/would)

B Rewrite these sentences, choosing a modal verb from the brackets to make the meaning less certain.

1. We will sell lots of Cream of Carrot again. (must/should)
2. We will run out of locusts. (might/must)
3. The food must be ready by now. (ought to/can't)

C Put the following sentences in the past.

1. The customers can see the picture of the dish.
2. He says he will pick up the food for next week.
3. The food should be ready to pick up.

> **Remember**
>
> To refer to the past, we use 'could' instead of 'can' and 'would' instead of 'will'. With other modals we usually use the following form: modal + have + past participle.
>
> *Examples*: She could speak English. They should have arrived yesterday.

Use of English

More modals

We can also use modal verbs to give advice and suggestions, to give permission, to say something is not allowed, to criticise someone's actions and to show that we regret something in the past.

advice and **suggestions**	should/shouldn't, ought to/ought not to, could, might
	Examples: If you're not well, you **ought to** see a doctor. We **could** eat at the restaurant this evening if you like.
permission / not allowed	*permission*: can, may, might *not allowed*: can't, may not, mustn't
	Examples: You **can** leave early today if you want to. **May** I borrow your phone? You **mustn't** use your phones in class.
criticism and **regret**	could/should/shouldn't/might + have + past participle
	Examples: You **should have done** more work. I **shouldn't have told** him that.

Using modals

A Fill the gaps in the following sentences using a modal verb from the box below.

> can't   should   shouldn't   may

1. Do you think I _____ order the locusts?
2. I _____ have eaten so much Cream of Carrot.
3. Customers _____ pay online if they wish.
4. You _____ leave the restaurant without paying.

B Rewrite the following sentences using a suitable modal verb. The first one has been done for you.

1. Customers are allowed to choose a starter, main course and dessert.

   Customers may choose a starter, main course and dessert.

2. I advise you to try the Lemon Locusts.
3. I wish I hadn't ordered the Seaweed and Grass Bake.
4. Customers are not allowed to enter the kitchen.

C Think of two things you wish you had done or regret about the past and then complete the following two sentences with your own words.

1. I should have _____
2. I shouldn't have _____

Speaking

Future foods

Many people think that we might not have enough food in the future to feed a growing population.

Word builder

Use words from the Glossary to complete the following paragraph.

Scientists _____ that rising temperatures will mean that it will become more difficult to grow important _____ such as wheat in the future. Scientists are _____ new ways to grow and make food, for example growing meat or fish in a _____, and developing seeds that can grow even in times of flood or _____.

Glossary

crops plants grown for use as food

drought a long time without water

laboratory a room used for scientific work

predict say that something will happen

researching finding information

Speaking about future foods

Look at the pictures and questions below and then discuss the questions on page 131 in groups.

Can pills ever replace food?

Could robots become responsible for growing, buying or preparing our food?

What do you think supermarkets will be like in the future?

What kind of food could there be on other planets?

Speaking

1. What do the pictures on page 130 show?
2. How could the way we eat change in the future?
3. Would you be willing to live on another planet if we could grow food there for the future? Discuss the advantages and the disadvantages of moving to another planet.

💬 Class competition

You are going to have a class competition. In small groups, you are going to design an advertisement for a new food. Everybody in the group must take part in the advertisement.

First decide what kind of advertisement you will make (e.g. poster, leaflet, television advertisement, radio advertisement). You will need to include:

- a description of your new food
- the way to serve it and examples of meals it can be used in
- where you can buy it and how much it costs
- how it was found/invented/developed
- what the advantages of your new food are.

Present your advertisement to the class. When you have listened to all the groups, vote for the best advertisement of a new food.

⭐ Challenge

One idea about food for the future is to use all available land (such as gardens or rooftops) to farm. The counter-argument to this might be that we should not farm all available land as that would have consequences for the environment. Work in a small group to brainstorm arguments for and against the following question: 'Should we farm on forest and grassland?'

Reading corner

📖 Reading corner: New discovery

You are going to read two fictional texts about the idea that pills might one day replace meals. The first is a blog and the second is the diary extract of the scientist who made the discovery. As you are reading, think about how the opinions of the writers are different.

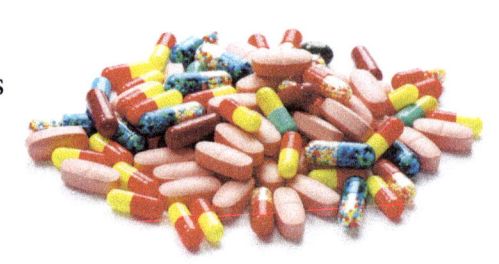

Can you imagine a time when you didn't have to programme your computer to create meals all the time? Well, I think you are going to love this new discovery!

Scientists have discovered that our favourite meals can be contained in pills.

One researcher, said: "The results were amazing. I tried one pink pill called 'Soya and Sunflower'. Not only was it tasty, but it's just so healthy – full of essential vitamins and minerals."

More details will follow next month – follow my blog to find out more.

POSTED BY Zina on 14.7.3040   20000876 followers

Saturday 14th July 3040

I am writing this in the middle of the night, as I just cannot sleep. I am full of doubt and worry. I cannot imagine that anyone will be interested in my new discovery of the food pill. I mean, all of the pleasure of eating will be taken away! Can something that people normally take as medicine replace the joy of eating good food? Who will ever consider not eating again or programming their computer? Why did I ever think that this discovery would give me worldwide success? It will be the end of my career as a scientist!

Understanding

Answer the following questions.

1. What is the blogger's opinion of the discovery?
2. How does the blogger encourage her readers to read her next blog?
3. Why does the scientist feel that the food pill will not be successful?
4. What did the scientist hope the discovery would bring?

Writing workshop

Writing food blogs

You are going to write two imaginative blogs about a meal that you have eaten in the future. One blog must be very positive and the other must be extremely negative.

Planning

For each blog, think about the following questions:
- What is the meal? Be as imaginative as possible.
- What does it look like?
- What does it taste like?
- What does it feel like?
- What does it smell like?

Drafting

Remember that one blog must be positive and one must be negative. For each one, think of powerful adjectives and adverbs to use.

Editing and redrafting

Swap your blogs with a partner. What has worked well and what needs changing?

Remember

Remember to experiment with vocabulary. Choose the best words to engage the reader.

Challenge

Can you replace five words in each blog with five more interesting or powerful words? Use a thesaurus to help extend your vocabulary.

Progress assessment

Progress check

Answer the following questions.

1. How many people are there on Earth, according to the article on page 122? (1 mark)

2. What are three benefits of dulse, according to the marine scientist quoted in the article? (3 marks)

3. What will happen in 35 years' time, according to the article? (1 mark)

4. Which of the following has the closest meaning to the word 'prediction'.
   a a guess   b something that people say might happen in the future   (1 mark)

5. Fill the gaps in the following sentences with the correct future form from the brackets.
   a They're _____ cook some seaweed. (will/going to)
   b I'm _____ dinner at a new restaurant tonight. (having/will have)
   c We'll _____ between 7 and 9 o'clock. (going to be eating/be eating)
   d The seaweed is _____ served with noodles. (going to be/will be)   (4 marks)

6. In Track 8.1, which course do Zach and Boni keep the same? Choose the correct answer.
   a the starters   b the main courses   c the desserts   (1 mark)

7. Choose the correct words from a–f to complete the following speech from Track 8.1.
   People just …(a)… understand that the …(b)… would be greater than food …(c)… and they simply didn't act in time. …(d)…, people thought they had more …(e)… to find and develop new …(f)…
   a did   didn't
   b production   population
   c production   population
   d In the future In the past
   e time   chance
   f foods   restaurants   (6 marks)

8. Fill in the gaps with a suitable modal verb from the brackets.
   a _____ I help you decide what to order? (Ought to/Shall/Would)
   b I'm not sure, but I _____ try some dulse. (can/should/might)
   c Kitchen staff _____ leave the fridge door open. (mustn't/won't/ought)
   d I _____ have eaten so much. (should/shouldn't/will)   (4 marks)

9. Name two differences between a blog and a diary extract. (2 marks)

10. Name two ways the opinions of the blogger and the scientist are different. (2 marks)

(Total: 25 marks)

134

Progress assessment

Progress assessment

		😊	😐	😟
Reading skills	I can understand implied meaning in texts.	○	○	○
	I can recognise a writer's attitude or opinion.	○	○	○
	I can work out meaning from the context.	○	○	○
	I can recognise inconsistencies in arguments.	○	○	○
Use of English skills	I can use future forms.	○	○	○
	I can use modal forms.	○	○	○
Listening skills	I can work out meaning from the context.	○	○	○
	I can recognise typical features when someone is speaking.	○	○	○
Speaking skills	I can explain advantages and disadvantages of ideas, plans and arrangements.	○	○	○
	I can think of other ways to say something if I have gaps in my knowledge.	○	○	○
Writing skills	I can develop clear arguments supported with reasons, examples and evidence.	○	○	○
	I can use the appropriate layout for a range of genres.	○	○	○

✓ Action plan

Reading: I need to _____

Use of English: I need to _____

Listening: I need to _____

Speaking: I need to _____

Writing: I need to _____

I would like to know more about _____

9 Communication in the past

Explore
- how people communicated in the past
- how pigeons were used to send messages

Collaborate
- to choose a classic typewriter
- to discuss a group design

Create
- a design for a postage stamp
- a lesson poem

Engage
- with a salesperson
- with poetry

Reflect
- on *if only/I wish* and relative clauses
- on phrasal and prepositional verbs

In this chapter you will:

> Words are but pictures of our thoughts.
> John Dryden, poet

> My belief is that communication is the best way to create strong relationships.
> Jada Pinkett Smith, actress

> Someone, somewhere wants a letter from you.
> British Post Office, 1960s

Communication in the past

🗨 Thinking ahead

1. How do you communicate with friends? List as many different ways as you can. Then compare your list with that of a partner.
2. How many of these ways would your grandparents have used when they were your age?
3. How would friends have communicated 100 years ago? What about even longer ago than that?

🧩 Word builder

Use words from the word box to complete the sentences below.

method   ancient   communicate   information   telegraph

1. It is often fast to find _____ on the Internet, but library books can be more reliable.
2. The Parthenon in Athens was built by the _____ Greeks.
3. The _____, a system for sending messages along a wire, was invented in the 19th century.
4. He had a simple _____ for cooking a vegetable curry.
5. Texting was Nadia's favourite way to _____.

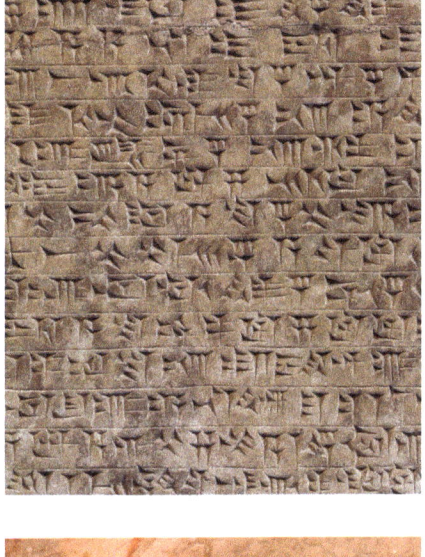

💬 Speaking about communication

Discuss the following questions with a partner.

1. How do you prefer to keep in touch with friends and family? Does it make a difference who the person is? For example, would you communicate with your best friend in a different way from the way you would use for your grandparents?
2. Why is good communication important?

Reading

📖 Pigeon post

One method of communication that was first used over 2,000 years ago is by pigeon. Read the article about this ancient postal service and then answer the questions that follow.

Pigeon post

'Pigeon post' is using pigeons to send messages. These birds, which are usually known as homing or carrier pigeons, are used because they can find their way home over long distances.

From earliest times, pigeons were **released** into the air as a sign of peace or to celebrate a special occasion. **Victors** of the ancient Olympic Games had the news sent home by carrier pigeon and over 2,000 years ago Julius Caesar is said to have used pigeons to send the news of his successes in battle back to Rome. Others who used pigeons to send messages included the ancient Persian and East Asian empires, with stories being told of how they **bred and trained** messenger birds. In the 19th century the international news firm, Reuters, sometimes used pigeons to send information about money markets in Europe.

Armies often used pigeons to send secret information during wartime. This continued even after the development of radio and telegraph, and laws were passed in many countries to protect the carrier pigeon.

Pigeons are no longer used to carry messages, but their skills are still seen in the international sport of pigeon racing. The pigeons are taken up to 1,000 kilometres away from where they are kept before being set free to fly home. The time each bird takes and the distance from the place it sets off from to its home are written down and the fastest bird home is the winner.

Glossary

bred and trained kept to produce young birds and prepared for a particular purpose

released set free

victors winners

Reading

Understanding

A Choose the correct answer to each of the following questions.

1. How were pigeons used at the ancient Olympic Games?
   - a to declare peace
   - b to start races
   - c to send news of the winners
2. Why did some countries pass laws about pigeons?
   - a to stop them being used
   - b to protect them
   - c to develop radio and telegraph
3. What are carrier pigeons used for today?
   - a to carry messages
   - b to measure distances
   - c to race against each other
4. Which pigeon wins the pigeon race?
   - a the one that flies home the fastest
   - b the one that flies the furthest
   - c the one that flies over 1,000 kilometres

B Choose the correct answer to each of the following questions.

1. What is another name for a carrier pigeon?
   - a pigeon post
   - b homing pigeon
   - c pigeon racing
2. What did Julius Caesar send by carrier pigeon?
   - a news of the Olympics
   - b news of his successes
   - c news of battles back in Rome
3. What did Reuters use carrier pigeons for?
   - a to send messages about wars
   - b to send money to market
   - c to send information about money

C Write a short paragraph on the subject 'Sending messages by pigeon'.

Challenge

Many other ways of sending messages were used in the past. Use a library or the internet to research and make notes on one of the following:

- smoke signals
- drum beating
- secret codes.

Use your notes to write a paragraph about the subject, then share your information in small groups.

139

Use of English

'If only' and 'wish'

We use 'if only' and 'wish (that)' to talk about things that we would like to change or things we would like to be different.

To talk about regrets and to express wishes about things that have already happened, we can use **if only** or **wish (that) + past perfect (had + past participle)**.

Examples: **She wishes (that) she hadn't forgotten** to post that letter.

If only I had listened more carefully.

We also use **if only** or **wish (that)** with **could have + past participle** to talk about things in the past that we wish had been possible or that we could have been able to do.

Examples: **I wish I could have been** there.

If only they could have arrived earlier.

Using 'if only' and 'wish'

A Complete the following sentences with past perfect forms of the verbs in the word box.

| fly | tell | receive | remember |

1. If only I _____ to send that email yesterday.
2. He wishes his pigeon _____ faster.
3. If only they _____ the message sooner.
4. I wish he _____ me the news himself.

Remember

To talk about present situations, we use 'if only' or 'wish (that)' + past simple.
Examples: If only I knew what to do. He wishes (that) his friend was here.

B Rewrite the following sentences replacing the verbs that are underlined with forms that express regrets or wishes about the past. The first one has been done for you.

1. She wishes she <u>knew</u> what was in the letter.

   She wishes she had known what was in the letter.

2. I wish I <u>believed</u> what he said on the phone.
3. If only you <u>could see</u> the pigeons set off.
4. She wishes she <u>could stay</u> a bit longer.

C Complete the following sentences so they are true for you.

1. I wish I had _____
2. If only I hadn't _____
3. I wish I could have _____

Use of English

Relative pronouns and relative clauses

We use **relative clauses** to give more information about a person or thing in a sentence. Relative clauses usually begin with a **relative pronoun**, such as 'who', 'whose', 'whom', 'which' or 'that'.

Examples: The pigeon **that flies fastest** wins the race.

Pigeons, **which are closely related to doves**, often used to carry messages.

The owner **whose pigeon wins the race** is given a prize.

When a relative pronoun is the object of the clause, we often leave it out.

Example: Where is the book **(that) I lent you**?

When a verb in a relative clause needs a preposition, we usually put the preposition at the end of the relative clause and we often leave out the relative pronoun. In formal writing, we sometimes put the preposition before the relative pronoun.

Examples: The news **(which)** he was waiting **for** has finally arrived.

The news **for which** he was waiting has finally arrived.

Using relative pronouns and relative clauses

A Complete the following sentences with a suitable relative pronoun. More than one answer may be possible.

1. Julius Caesar, _____ was a Roman soldier and politician, used pigeons to send news back to Rome.
2. The message _____ the pigeon was carrying was secret.
3. Carrier pigeons are birds _____ can find their way home over long distances.
4. Racing pigeons, _____ homes are called lofts, can fly very long distances.

B Rewrite the following sentences, changing the position of the preposition to make the sentences less formal. The first one has been done for you.

1. Is she the person to whom you sent the email?

   Is she the person who you sent the email to?
2. The race in which his pigeon is flying started yesterday.
3. The letter for which I was waiting has just arrived.
4. From where did the pigeon fly home?

Remember

- We use 'who', 'whose', 'whom' and 'that' to refer to people and 'which', 'that' and 'whose' to talk about animals and things.
- We sometimes use 'where', 'when' and 'why' to introduce relative clauses.
- We use 'whom' instead of 'who' after a preposition.

141

Listening

Typewriters for sale

Word builder

Use the words or phrases from the word box to complete the sentences below.

complicated   electronic   matching   up-to-date

1. Our new curtains and cushions are made from _____ material.
2. The design for the new science centre is very modern and _____.
3. The sisters often played games on _____ devices like phones and tablets, but they also liked playing board games together.
4. When you are learning a new sport, the rules can seem very _____.

Track 9.1: Typewriters for sale

You are going to listen to a salesperson talking about historic typewriters he has for sale. Read the words and their meanings in the Glossary and then listen to the recording.

Glossary

auto-correcting able to correct mistakes itself

classic popular for a long time and of high quality

feature an important part of something

illustrated with pictures

portable can be carried

traditional following the customs or style of the past

Listening

Understanding

A Choose the correct answer to each of the following questions.

1. What is the salesperson trying to sell?
   a classic typewriters
   b computer lessons
   c beautiful letters

2. What is the colour of the traditional typewriter?
   a green
   b blue
   c black

3. What is offered with every model?
   a case
   b instruction book
   c auto-correcting feature

4. Which of the following could be described as 'portable'?
   a a car
   b a smartphone
   c a cinema

B Listen to the recording again. Why does the salesperson think people might want to buy one of his typewriters? Give two reasons.

C Write a sentence each on the three typewriters for sale, showing how they are different from one another.

Buying a typewriter

You are interested in buying one of the typewriters for sale. Which one would you choose? Why? What are the advantages and disadvantages of each? Take turns in a small group to explain your choice.

Use of English

Phrasal verbs

Phrasal verbs are made up of a main verb and a particle, such as 'in', 'out', 'over', 'up', 'away' or 'off'. Many phrasal verbs can be used without an object.

Examples: He has just **woken up**. We have decided to **eat out**.

When a phrasal verb has an object, the particle can usually come before or after the object.

Examples: I **wrote down** your number. (subject + verb + particle + object)

I **wrote** your number **down**. (subject + verb + object + particle)

If the object is a pronoun, the pronoun must come before the particle.

Example: I **wrote it down**. (not 'I wrote down it')

Phrasal verbs that are followed by prepositions always have an object. The object comes after the preposition.

Example: I have **run out of time**.

Using phrasal verbs

A Use words from the word box to complete the following email.

> get   up   signed   find   in

I would like to _____ out about the typewriters you have for sale. Have the prices gone _____ since last year? If I decide to buy one, should I fill _____ an order form? I would be grateful if you could _____ back to me soon, as I have just _____ up for some typing lessons!

Remember

Phrasal verbs are made up of two words – a main verb and a particle, such as 'in', 'out', 'over', 'up', 'away' or 'off'. Together the words often have a different meaning from the verb on its own.
Example: give + up = give up (I have given up learning the piano.)

B Rewrite the following sentences using the correct form of a phrasal verb from the box instead of the verbs that are underlined.

> come out   look up   pick up

1. I <u>searched for</u> the word in a dictionary.
2. The book <u>was published</u> last year.
3. Have you <u>collected</u> the parcel from the post office?

C Write three sentences of your own using the phrasal verbs 'run out', 'leave behind' and 'hand out'.

Use of English

Prepositional verbs

Prepositional verbs are formed with a verb and a preposition such as 'to', 'on', 'of', 'with' or 'for'. Unlike phrasal verbs, prepositional verbs always have an object, which comes after the preposition. The object can be a noun, a noun phrase, a pronoun or the –ing form of a verb.

Examples: Have you **heard from** Marco?

I have **applied for** a new job.

She always **looks after** you.

I am **thinking about** buying a typewriter.

Unlike phrasal verbs, prepositional verbs cannot be separated. We cannot put the object between the verb and the preposition. (We cannot say 'She always looks you after.')

Using prepositional verbs

A Insert a suitable preposition to complete these sentences.

1. Does this book belong _____ you?
2. A keyboard mainly consists _____ a set of buttons called keys.
3. I can't decide whether to buy a typewriter. It depends _____ the price.
4. I have decided to go _____ the portable typewriter.

B Put the words in the right order in the following sentences.

1. late/apologised/arriving/for/I
2. agreed/plans/to/my/he
3. typing/my/keep/I/practising/on/will
4. my/I/exam/passing/in/succeeded

C Write four sentences of your own using the following prepositional verbs.

> deal with   believe in   recover from   complain about

145

Speaking

Postal services

People have used postal services to deliver letters and parcels for hundreds of years. This has sometimes been celebrated on postage stamps, as the examples here show.

Speaking

Postal services

In pairs, look at each of the stamps in turn and discuss the following questions.

1. Can you work out where each one is from?
2. What is shown in the picture?
3. What kind of transport is being used?
4. What do you find especially interesting in the picture?

Word builder

Use words or phrases from the word box to complete the paragraph below.

| post | letter | letterbox | airmail |

Rashid sent a _____ to his family in Bahrain. As he wanted it to arrive quickly, he decided to send it by _____. They do not have a _____ at the family home, but collect their _____ from a nearby PO box.

Design a postage stamp

You have been asked to design a stamp for your country celebrating the postal service of your region. In a small group, discuss what you think should be included. For example:

- something from the past or the latest technology
- the transport used
- an unusual delivery
- a particular place
- a town or country setting
- something eye-catching.

Now work in your groups to draw the design of the stamp and prepare a short talk to give to the class. You will need to explain what your stamp celebrates and how it does this. Make sure that everyone in the group has a chance to take part.

Reading corner

📖 Reading corner: 'The Postage Stamp Lesson'

You are going to read a poem in which a postage stamp is used as an example to follow. Read the poem and then answer the questions.

The Postage Stamp Lesson

There was a little postage stamp
No bigger than your thumb;
But still it **stuck right to** the job
Until the work was done.

They **licked** it and they **pounded** it
'Til it would make you sick;
And the more it took a-lickin'
The better it would stick.

Let's all be like the postage stamp
In playing life's **rough** game;
And just keep on a-stickin'
Tho' we **hang our heads in shame**.

The stamp stuck to the letter
'Till it saw it safely through;
There's no one can do better
Let's keep sticking and be true.

Anonymous (from http://poetrynook.com/poem/postage-stamp-lesson)

Understanding

Answer the following questions.

1. What is the postage stamp's 'job'?
2. When does that job finish, according to the poem?
3. 'To lick' someone is an old-fashioned way of saying you have beaten them. How does this add to our understanding of the poem?
4. Sum up in your own words the lesson of the poem.

Glossary

hang our heads in shame are ashamed or embarrassed

licked moved your tongue across something

pounded kept hitting

rough hard, difficult

stuck right to kept going with something

⭐ Challenge

Track 9.2 Listen to the reading of the poem 'The Night Mail' and follow the transcript. The poem tells the story of the train carrying the day's post from London to Edinburgh. As you listen, see if you can hear the rhythmic sound of the steam train. Sometimes the journey is smooth and fast and at others the journey is uphill. In pairs, practise reading parts of the poem to one another.

Choose one of the letters mentioned in the poem and write the message you think it might have contained. You could even try to put it in the form of a short poem.

Writing workshop

✏️ Writing a lesson poem

'The Postage Stamp Lesson' is an example of a simple poem that has a deeper meaning. The way the stamp stays on the envelope is taken by the poet as something for us to follow. The poem encourages us not to give up when we find things difficult, but to stick at what we are doing until the job is done.

You are going to write a poem or short story that gives advice or an example to follow.

Getting started

Begin by thinking of an object or an event that we can learn from.

Some ideas to help you get started:

- a clock – never hurried or slow
- a ruler – keeps straight and guides others
- a race – the one who starts quickly isn't necessarily the one who finishes first
- a torch – does not do anything until it's switched on but can then be used to show the way
- a spider making a web.

Writing a description

Choose one of the ideas above or think of one of your own and write a simple description of the object and what it does. Finish with the lesson we can learn from it. Read 'The Postage Stamp Lesson' again, noticing how the description of what the stamp does is set out.

Writing and proofreading your poem

Now try turning your description into a poem, or if you prefer, tell a story about it. When you have completed your writing, proofread what you have written for accuracy. Then compare your work with that of your partner and discuss how they could be improved.

Progress check

Answer the following questions.

1. How was news of who had won events in the ancient Olympic Games sent home? Choose the correct answer.
   - a by runners
   - b by pigeon
   - c by smoke signal   (1 mark)

2. In delivering pigeon post where do the pigeons fly to? Choose the correct answer.
   - a their home
   - b the nearest post office
   - c the city   (1 mark)

3. Write a sentence to explain how carrier pigeons are used today.   (2 marks)

4. Fill the gaps in the following sentences with a suitable preposition or relative pronoun.
   - a A postage stamp is a small piece of paper _____ is stuck on a letter or parcel.
   - b The envelope that the address is written _____ does not have a stamp.
   - c The person the letter was sent _____ has moved out.   (3 marks)

5. Choose the correct words from a–f to complete the following paragraph about what happens in Track 9.1.

   The salesperson was selling old …(a)… which he said were a piece of …(b)… . They were …(c)… of famous machines from the …(d)… . They had been brought up to date and so were …(e)… to use. Each model had its own instruction book to help you become an …(f)… .

a	typewriters	books	b	furniture	history
c	copies	choices	d	shop	past
e	hard	easy	f	expert	expect

   (6 marks)

6. Name two colours that the typewriters were made in.   (2 marks)

7. Match the phrasal verbs on the left with their meanings on the right.

get up	to continue to do something
keep on	to arrive somewhere
end up	to wake up and get out of bed

   (3 marks)

8. Name four forms of transport shown on the postage stamps on page 146.   (4 marks)

9. The postage stamp in the poem 'The Postage Stamp Lesson' was described as being the same size as what?   (1 mark)

10. What good example does the postage stamp give?   (2 marks)

(Total: 25 marks)

Progress assessment

Progress assessment

		😊	😐	😟
Reading skills	I can understand specific points in a text.	○	○	○
	I can understand implied meaning in texts.	○	○	○
Use of English skills	I can use *if only/I wish* and relative clauses.	○	○	○
	I can use phrasal and prepositional verbs.	○	○	○
Listening skills	I can work out meaning from the context.	○	○	○
	I can understand most of the implied meaning when someone is speaking.	○	○	○
Speaking skills	I can explain my own point of view.	○	○	○
	I can work with others to negotiate, agree and organise plans in class.	○	○	○
Writing skills	I can use the correct style and register for a range of genres.	○	○	○
	I can compose, edit and proofread written work.	○	○	○

✓ Action plan

Reading: I need to _____

Use of English: I need to _____

Listening: I need to _____

Speaking: I need to _____

Writing: I need to _____

I would like to know more about _____

Grammar reference

Forming comparative and superlative adjectives

For information on the use of comparative and superlative adjectives, see Unit 2 page 29.

Adjective	Rule	Examples
one syllable (most)	add –er or –est	warm → warmer → warmest
one syllable ending with a silent –e	drop the –e and add –er or –est	large → larger → largest
one syllable ending with consonant + vowel + consonant	double the final consonant and add –er or –est*	big → bigger → biggest
one or two syllables ending with –y	change –y to –i and add –er or –est	lucky → luckier → luckiest
two syllables, not ending with y (many)	'more' or 'most' + adjective**	careful → more careful → most careful
adjectives with three syllables or more	'more' or 'most' + adjective	interesting → more interesting → most interesting

* Exception: We do not double the final consonant when an adjective ends in –w or –y (examples: slower/slowest, greyer/greyest).

** With some two-syllable adjectives, we can use 'more/most' or add '–er/–est' (examples: cleverer/more clever, simpler/more simple, politer/more polite).

Forming comparative and superlative adverbs

For information on the use of comparative and superlative adverbs, see Unit 2 page 33.

Adverb	Rule	Examples
adverbs ending with –ly	use 'more' or 'most' in front of the adverb	carefully → more carefully → most carefully
short adverbs that do not end with –ly	add –er or –est if the adverb ends in –e, drop the –e and add –er or –est	fast → faster → fastest late → later → latest

Grammar reference

Irregular comparatives and superlatives

These common adjectives and adverbs have irregular comparative and superlative forms.

Adjective/adverb	Comparative	Superlative
good	better	best
well	better	best
bad	worse	worst
badly	worse	worst
ill	worse	worst
much	more	most
little (quantity)	less	least
far	farther/further	farthest/furthest

Forming verbs + –ing

Verb	Rule	Examples
most verbs	add –ing	look → looking
verbs ending with consonant + –e	remove the –e and add –ing	move → moving
verbs ending with –ee	add –ing	agree → agreeing
verbs ending with consonant + vowel + consonant	double the final consonant and add –ing*	stop → stopping
verbs ending with –ie	change –ie to –y and add –ing	lie → lying

* Exceptions: We do not double a final –w or –x (examples: flow → flowing, fix → fixing). We do not double the consonant when the last syllable is not stressed (example: order → ordering).

Forming verbs + ed

Verb	Rule	Examples
most verbs	add –ed	look → looked
verbs ending with –e or –ee	add –d	move → moved agree → agreed
verbs ending in consonant + y	change –y to –i and add –ed	study → studied
verbs ending in consonant + vowel + consonant	double the final consonant and add –ed*	stop → stopped prefer → preferred

* Exception: We do not double the consonant when the last syllable is not stressed (example: order → ordered).

Grammar reference

Verb forms

Present simple

See Unit 4 pages 60–61, Unit 5 page 76 and Unit 8 page 125.

Positive	I/you/we/they walk	He/she/it walks
Negative	I/you/we/they don't walk	He/she/it doesn't walk
Question	Do I/you/we/they walk?	Does he/she/it walk?

Present continuous

See Unit 4 page 64 and Unit 8 page 125.

Positive	I am walking	He/she/it is walking	You/we/they are walking
Negative	I'm not walking	He/she/it isn't walking	You/we/they aren't walking
Question	Am I walking?	Is he/she/it walking?	Are you/we/they walking?

Past simple

See Unit 4 pages 60–61, Unit 5 page 76 and Unit 6 page 93.

Positive	I/you/he/she/it/we/they walked
Negative	I/you/he/she/it/we/they didn't walk
Question	Did I/you/he/she/it/we/they walk?

Past continuous

See Unit 4 page 65.

Positive	I/he/she/it was walking	You/we/they were walking
Negative	I/he/she/it wasn't walking	You/we/they weren't walking
Question	Was I/he/she/it walking?	Were you/we/they walking?

Grammar reference

Present perfect simple

See Unit 6 page 92.

Positive	I/you/we/they have walked	He/she/it has walked
Negative	I/you/we/they haven't walked	He/she/it hasn't walked
Question	Have I/you/we/they walked?	Has he/she/it walked?

Present perfect continuous

See Unit 6 page 92.

Positive	I/you/we/they have been walking	He/she/it has been walking
Negative	I/you/we/they haven't been walking	He/she/it hasn't been walking
Question	Have I/you/we/they been walking?	Has he/she/it been walking?

Past perfect simple

See Unit 6 page 93.

Positive	I/you/he/she/it/we/they had walked
Negative	I/you/he/she/it/we/they hadn't walked
Question	Had I/you/he/she/it/we/they walked?

Past perfect continuous

See Unit 6 page 93.

Positive	I/you/he/she/it/we/they had been walking
Negative	I/you/he/she/it/we/they hadn't been walking
Question	Had I/you/he/she/it/we/they been walking?

Future continuous

See Unit 8 page 125.

Positive	I/you/he/she/it/we/they will be walking
Negative	I/you/he/she/it/we/they won't be walking
Question	Will I/you/he/she/it/we/they be walking?

Use of English: Glossary

abstract noun a noun that refers to an idea, quality or concept that cannot be seen or touched (examples: happiness, truth, beauty). *See also* concrete noun.

active verbs are active when the subject of the sentence (the agent) does the action. (Example: He *cleaned* the windows this morning.) *See also* passive.

adjective a word that gives more information about a noun or adds to its meaning. Adjectives are often used in front of a noun. (Example: They live in a *big* house.) Adjectives can also be used after verbs such as 'be', 'feel' and 'look'. (Examples: He is *hungry*. She feels *happy*.)

adverb a word that is used to give more information about a verb, adjective or another adverb. (Examples: She speaks English *well*. He is *very* tall. He spoke *really* loudly.)

auxiliary verb a verb ('be', 'have' or 'do') that is used with a main verb to form tenses, passive forms and questions. (Examples: She *is* eating her lunch. She *has* eaten her lunch. Her lunch *was* eaten. *Did* she eat her lunch?) *See also* modal verb.

causative form a form such as 'have/get something done' used when we want to talk about something that someone else does for us or another person. (Example: I *get my hair cut* every three months.)

clause a group of words that contains a verb and usually some other words, too. Clauses form part of a sentence or may be complete sentences on their own. (Example: I went to school.) *See also* main clause, conditional clause, relative clause.

command an order to do something. (Example: Stop talking.) *See also* imperative.

comparative the form of an adjective or adverb that is used when comparing things. (Examples: You are *taller* than me. Mara works *harder* than Jamal.)

compound adjective an adjective made up of two or more words. (Examples: She is a *prize-winning* writer. He bought a *second-hand* car.)

compound noun a noun made up of two or more words (examples: haircut, swimming pool).

concrete noun a noun that refers to something that can be seen or touched (examples: school, house, apple). *See also* abstract noun.

conditional clause a clause that describes something that must happen in order for something else to happen. Conditional clauses usually begin with 'if' or 'unless'. (Examples: *If I see her*, I will tell her what you said. *Unless it stops raining*, we will not go for a walk.)

conjunction a word that is used to link words or parts of a sentence, such as 'and', 'but', 'since' and 'as'.

continuous form a verb form used to describe an action that continues over a period of time. We make continuous forms using a form of the verb 'be' with the present participle of the main verb. To change the tense, we change the form of 'be'. (Examples: I *am eating* my lunch. He *was reading* his book. She *has been doing* her homework. They *will be arriving* soon.)

contraction a shortened form of a word or group of words. An apostrophe is used to show where letters have been missed out (examples: I'm [I am], you're [you are]).

countable noun a noun that refers to something that can be counted. Countable nouns have singular and plural forms (examples: planet/planets, book/books).

determiner a word that is used before a noun and forms part of a noun phrase (examples: a/an, the, this, some, many, this, that, these, much, your).

direct speech the words spoken by someone and quoted in writing. To indicate direct speech, we use inverted commas, or speech marks. (Example: She said, "*I will see you tomorrow.*") *See also* reported speech.

embedded question a question that is included in a statement. (Example: I don't know what time it is.)

future a verb form used to refer to something that has not yet happened. To talk about something that has been arranged in the future, we often use the present simple or present continuous. (Examples: My piano lesson *is* at 4 o'clock. I *am having* a piano lesson tomorrow.) Other future forms include 'will' and 'be going to' and the future continuous.

future continuous *See* continuous form.

gerund a present participle of a verb (–ing form) when it is used as a noun. (Example: I like *reading*.)

imperative a verb form that expresses a command or instruction. (Examples: *Be* quiet. *Close* the door.)

indirect question a question that is included in another question. (Example: Could you tell me what time it is?)

infinitive the basic form of a verb (examples: read, be). The infinitive with 'to' is 'to' + base form (examples: to read, to be).

Use of English: Glossary

–ing form the present participle form of a verb ending in –ing. We use the –ing form in continuous forms. (Example: I *am reading* a book.) We also use –ing forms as nouns (gerunds). (Examples: I like *reading. Reading* is relaxing.) We also some use –ing forms as adjectives. (Example: This is an *exciting* book.)

irregular an irregular word does not follow the normal rules. Irregular nouns do not have plurals that end in –s (examples: man → men, child → children). An irregular verb does not have a past tense and past participle that end in –ed (examples: go → went/gone, be → was/were/been). *See also* regular.

main clause a group of words that contains a subject and a verb and can stand alone as a complete sentence. Every sentence contains at least one main clause. (Example: *Mara was reading the book* that she borrowed from the library.)

main verb the verb that expresses the main meaning in a clause (unlike an auxiliary verb). Main verbs can be used with or without an auxiliary verb. (Examples: I *read* a good book last week. I am *reading* a good book.)

modal verb a verb that we can use with another verb to express ideas such as ability, advice, possibility, permission, etc. The main modal verbs are: can, could, may might, must, ought (to), shall, should, will and would. (Examples: He *can* play the piano very well. You *should* wear a coat.)

noun a word that refers to a person, thing or idea. *See also* abstract noun, compound noun, concrete noun, countable noun, noun phrase, uncountable noun.

noun phrase a phrase that contains a noun. Noun phrases can contain determiners and other words that give more information about the noun (example: the blue shirt that I was wearing yesterday).

object a noun or pronoun that is the person or thing that is affected by a verb. (Example: He kicked *the ball* into the goal.) *See also* subject.

participle *See* –ing form, past participle.

particle a word, such as an adverb, that is added to a verb to make a phrasal verb. (Example: The bus broke *down*.)

passive verbs are passive when the subject of the verb has the action done to it. (Example: The windows *were cleaned* last week.) *See also* active.

past continuous *See* continuous form.

past participle a form of a verb that we use to make some past forms and passives. Regular verbs have past participles that end in –ed. (Example: He has *delivered* all the leaflets.) Irregular verbs have different forms. (Example: I have *sent* my friend a postcard.) Past participles are also used to form adjectives. (Examples: They have mended the *broken* window. The shop is *closed*.)

past perfect a verb form used to talk about the past. We use the past perfect simple (had + past participle) to talk about an event that happened before another event in the past. (Example: The film *had* already *started* when we arrived.) We use the past perfect continuous (had been + present participle) to talk about events in the past that began before another event in the past and were continuing up to that time. (Example: I *had been learning* English for a year when I went to my new school.)

past simple a verb form that we make by adding –ed to regular verbs. Irregular verbs have different forms. We use the past simple to talk about actions or events that happened in the past. (Example: I *called* him yesterday.)

past tense *See* continuous form, past perfect, past simple, present perfect, tense.

perfect *See* present perfect and past perfect.

phrasal verb a verb made up of a verb and a particle such as 'to', 'in' 'up', 'off', 'down', etc. A phrasal verb often has a different meaning from the verb alone. When a phrasal verb has an object, it can usually come before or after the particle. (Examples: My car *broke down*. He *put* his coat *on*. He *put on* his coat.)

phrase a group of words that forms a unit within a clause. (Examples: Have you seen *my blue coat*? I put the book *on the table*.)

plural the form of a word that we use to refer to more than one person or thing (examples: books, they).

preposition a word such as 'at', 'into', 'on' or 'for' that we use before a noun or pronoun to show place, direction, time, method, etc. (Examples: The book is *on* the desk; He walked *across* the street. I will see you *at* 6 o'clock. I went to Japan *by* plane.)

prepositional phrase a group of words that consists of a preposition and a noun, noun phrase or pronoun

Use of English: Glossary

and does not contain a verb or a subject (examples: by tomorrow, in the evening, for you).

prepositional verb a verb that is made up of a verb and a preposition. Prepositional verbs always have objects. (Examples: She *listened to* what her friend was saying. He cannot *do without* your help.)

present continuous See continuous form.

present participle See –ing form.

present perfect a verb form that we use to talk about past actions that connect to the present. We make the present perfect simple with a form of 'have' and the past participle of the main verb. (Example: I *have* already *read* this book.) The present perfect continuous is formed with 'have/has' + been + present participle. (Example: I *have been reading* a good book.)

present simple the form of a verb that we use to talk about things that are true in the present and actions that happen regularly in the present. We make the present simple with the base form of the verb. With 'he', 'she' and 'it' we add –s to the base form of regular verbs and many irregular verbs. (Examples: He *lives* in Hong Kong. I often *walk* to school.) We also use the present simple to talk about something that is fixed in the future. (Example: My lesson *starts* at 6 o'clock.)

present tense See present simple, present perfect, continuous form, tense.

pronoun a word that is used in place of a noun. Subject pronouns usually come before a verb (examples: I, you, he, she, it, we, they). Object pronouns come after the verb (examples: me, you, him, her, it, us, them). Relative pronouns connect relative clauses to main clauses in a sentence (examples: who, which, that). Possessive pronouns show who something belongs to (examples: mine, yours, his, hers, ours, theirs). Demonstrative pronouns refer to a particular person or thing (examples: this, that, these, those). Indefinite pronouns refer to people and things that are not specific (examples: somebody, everyone, anything). Reflexive pronouns are used when the subject and object of the verb are the same person or thing (examples: myself, yourself, themselves).

quantifier a word that expresses the quantity, number or amount of something (examples: all, both, many, several, lots of, little).

regular a word that follows normal rules. For example, regular nouns have plurals with –s and regular verbs have past participles ending in –ed.

relative clause a clause that gives information about someone or something in the main clause. A relative clause is usually connected to a main clause by a relative pronoun such as 'that', 'which', 'who' or 'where'. (Example: I read the book *that my friend lent me*.)

reported speech the words someone uses to report what someone has said. (Example: She said that she enjoyed the match.) See also direct speech.

singular the form of a word that we use to refer to one person or thing (examples: book, she).

statement a sentence that is not a question or a command. (Example: The match has just started.)

subject the person or thing that performs the action of a verb in a sentence. (Example: *He* kicked the ball into the goal.) See also object.

superlative the form of an adjective or adverb that is used when comparing things to express the idea of 'most' or 'least'. (Examples: He is the *tallest* student in the class. I arrived *earliest*. Of all of the students in the class, Ali plays football *least often*.)

syllable a word or part of a word that contains one vowel sound and usually one or more consonants before or after the vowel sound (example: meet [one syllable], meeting [two syllables 'meet' and 'ing']).

tense the form that a verb takes to show when something happened or when someone did something.

uncountable noun a noun that refers to something that we cannot count. Most uncountable nouns do not have a plural form (examples: water, information). See also countable noun.

verb a word that describes what someone or something does, or what happens (examples: look, read, seem, understand).

Index

present perfect continuous tense 92, 155
present perfect simple tense 92, 155
present simple tense 92, 125, 154
presentations 91
    group presentations 67, 83, 99
progress assessments
    arts and crafts 70–1
    communication in the past 150–1
    fitness trends 38–9
    food in the future 134–5
    friends and family 86–7
    global learning 102–3
    history around us 118–19
    natural landscapes 22–3
    working abroad 54–5
pronouns
    demonstrative pronouns 44
    indefinite pronouns 44
    reflexive pronouns 45
    relative pronouns 141

Q
quantifiers 17, 97
questions 76–7, 80
    indirect and embedded questions 81
    present continuous tense 64
    present simple and past simple tenses 76

R
reading corner
    Breaking the Jump 36
    Chinwe Roy 68
    Emma 84
    food in the future 132
    global learning 100
    'Light Bulb' 116
    'The Postage Stamp Lesson' 148–9
    travel diary 20
    working abroad 52
reflexive pronouns 45
relative clauses 141
relative pronouns 141
reported statements 80
Roy, Chinwe 68

S
speaking
    arts and crafts 57, 59, 66, 67
    communication in the past 137
    fitness trends 25, 31
    food in the future 121, 123
    friends and family 73, 79, 82–3
    global learning 89, 91, 98
    history around us 105, 111
    natural landscapes 9, 15, 18
    working abroad 41, 47
specific determiners 16
story writing 37, 85, 127
suffixes 12
superlative adjectives 29
    forming superlative adjectives 152
    irregular superlative adjectives 153
superlative adverbs 33
    forming superlative adverbs 152
    irregular superlative adverbs 153

T
thinking ahead
    arts and crafts 57
    communication in the past 137
    fitness trends 25
    food in the future 121
    friends and family 73
    global learning 89
    history around us 105
    natural landscapes 9
    working abroad 41, 46
time capsules 114

U
uncountable nouns 13, 17
understanding
    arts and crafts 59, 62–3, 68
    communication in the past 139, 148
    fitness trends 27, 31, 36
    food in the future 123, 126–7, 132
    friends and family 75, 78–9, 84
    global learning 91, 94–5, 100
    history around us 107, 111, 116
    natural landscapes 11, 15, 20
    working abroad 42–3, 46–7, 52

V
verbs
    active forms 60
    causative forms 61
    forming verbs + -ed 153
    forming verbs + -ing 153
    -ing verb forms 113
    -ing verb forms used as nouns 96
    modal verbs 128–9
    passive forms 60
    phrasal verbs 144
    prepositional verbs 145
    verbs followed by infinitives 112
Victoria Falls, Zambia-Zimbabwe border 10

W
Wallace, Harrison 94
'wish' 140
word builders
    arts and crafts 57, 67
    communication in the past 137, 142, 147
    fitness trends 25, 30
    food in the future 121, 130
    friends and family 73, 78
    global learning 89, 94
    history around us 105, 110, 115
    natural landscapes 9, 14, 19
    working abroad 41, 50
working abroad 40–1
    Ji-min's story 42
    living and working abroad 50
    preparing for work 51
    working in another country 46
    writing a formal email 47
    writing an informal email 43
writing workshops
    writing a biography 69
    writing a factual story 37
    writing a formal email 47, 91
    writing a formal letter 59
    writing a lesson poem 149
    writing a story 85
    writing a travel diary 21
    writing an acrostic poem 117
    writing an application for your dream job 53
    writing an informal email 43
    writing e-book cover 95
    writing e-book paragraph 95
    writing food blogs 133
    writing *The Great Hunger of 2040* 127

Index

A
abstract nouns 12
action plans 23, 55, 39, 71, 87, 103, 119, 135, 151
active verbs 60
adjectives 28, 96
    adjectives followed by infinitives 112
    comparative adjectives 29, 152
    compound adjectives 28
    irregular comparative and superlative adjectives 153
    superlative adjectives 29, 152
adverbs 32
    adverbs in sentences 32
    comparative adverbs 33, 152
    irregular comparative and superlative adverbs 153
    superlative adverbs 33, 152
Angel, Julie *Breaking the Jump* 36
arts and crafts 56–7
    different arts and crafts 66
    how Fivi's hobby became her business 62
    paper basket weaving 58–9
    writing a formal letter 59
    writing about Fivi's opinion 63
Atacama Desert, Chile 10
Austen, Jane *Emma* 84

B
biography writing 69
blog writing 133

C
causative verbs 61
challenges
    communication in the past 139, 148
    fitness trends 27, 28
    food in the future 123, 125, 127, 131, 133
    friends and family 75
    global learning 95
    history around us 107
    natural landscapes 11
    working abroad 43, 47, 48, 49
commands 80
communication in the past 136–7
    buying a typewriter 143
    design a postage stamp 147
    pigeon post 137–8
    postal services 146–7
    typewriters for sale 142–3
    writing a lesson poem 149
comparative adjectives 29
    forming comparative adjectives 152
    irregular comparative adjectives 153
comparative adverbs 33
    forming comparative adverbs 152
    irregular comparative adverbs 153
compound adjectives 28
compound nouns 12, 96
conjunctions 108–9
countable nouns 13, 17

D
demonstrative pronouns 44
determiners 16
digital technology 90

E
e-books 90
    writing e-book cover 95
    writing e-book paragraph 95
-ed verb forms 153
email 43, 47, 91
embedded questions 81
exchange programmes 99

F
fitness trends 24–5
    choosing a fitness trend 30–1
    colour running 26–7
    designing a poster 34
    fitness trends now and then 35
food in the future 120–1
    class competition 131
    conversation between two chefs in the year 3020 126–7
    finding foods for the future 122–3
    future foods 130–1
    writing food blogs 133
friends and family 72–3
    can you advise me, please? 78–9
    group discussion and presentation 83
    letters 74
    one big family? 82
    writing a story 85
future continuous tense 125, 155
future verb forms 124–5

G
general determiners 16
gerunds 96
getting something done 61
global learning 88–9
    exchange programmes 99
    how e-books can help to make a global community 90
    interview with Harrison Wallace 94
    presentations 91, 99
    writing a formal email 91
    writing an article to persuade 101
    writing e-book cover 95
    writing e-book paragraph 95
Global School Community 90
glossaries
    arts and crafts 58, 62, 68
    communication in the past 138, 142, 148
    fitness trends 26, 36
    food in the future 122, 126, 130
    friends and family 74, 84
    global learning 90, 95, 100
    history around us 106, 110, 116
    natural landscapes 10, 20
    use of English 156–9
    working abroad 42, 46, 52
Great Barrier Reef, Australia 10
group presentations 67, 83, 99
group research 99

H
having something done 61
history around us 104–5
    invention of light bulbs 110–11
    paper, pens and pencils 106
    time capsules 114, 115
    writing an acrostic poem 117

I
'if only' 140
indefinite pronouns 44
indirect questions 81
infinitives 112
-ing verb forms 113, 153
    -ing verb forms used as nouns 96
irregular comparative and superlative adjectives 153
irregular comparative and superlative adverbs 153

J
job applications 53

L
Lake Baikal, Siberia 10
letters 74
    letter writing 59

M
modal verbs 128–9

N
natural landscapes 8–9
    create an advertisement 19
    describing natural landscapes 18–19
    different landscapes 10–11
    The Wave, Arizona 14–15
nouns
    abstract nouns 12
    compound nouns 12, 96
    countable nouns 13, 17
    -ing verb forms used as nouns 96
    noun phrases 16, 97
    uncountable nouns 13, 17

P
paper 106
paper basket weaving 58–9
passive verbs 60
    past continuous tense 65
    present continuous tense 64
    present perfect simple tense 92
past continuous tense 65, 154
past perfect continuous tense 93, 155
past perfect simple tense 93, 155
past simple tense 92, 154
pencils 106
pens 106
phrasal verbs 144
pigeon post 137–8
poetry writing 117, 149
postal services 146–7
prepositional verbs 145
prepositions 48–9
present continuous tense 64, 125, 154